Port Elgin Ontario in Photos, Saving Our History One Photo at a Time

Photography
by Barbara Raué
2013

Series Name:
Cruising Ontario

Book 32: Port Elgin

Cover photo: 543 Mill Street, Port Elgin

Series Name: Cruising Ontario

Book 1: London
Book 2: Dundas
Book 3: Hamilton
Book 4: Oakville
Book 5: Chesley
Book 6: Stoney Creek
Book 7: Waterdown
Book 8: Owen Sound
Book 9: Mount Forest
Book 10: Dundalk
Book 11: Burford
Book 12: Waterford
Book 13: Drumbo
Book 14: Sheffield
Book 15: Tavistock
Book 16: Ancaster and Mount Hope
Book 17: Innerkip
Book 18: Brantford
Book 19: Burlington
Book 20: Guelph
Book 21: Ayr
Book 22: Erin
Book 23: Goderich
Book 24: Lucknow
Book 25: Paris
Book 26: Toronto
Book 27: Beaver Valley
Book 28: Collingwood
Book 29: Peterborough
Book 30: Orangeville Beginnings Part 1
Book 31: Orangeville Part 2 and Area
Book 32: Port Elgin
Book 33: Southampton
Book 34: Jarvis

Other Books by Barbara Raue

Coins of Gold

Arrows, Indians and Love

The Life and Times of Barbara
Volume 1: Inventions That Have Enhanced My Life
Volume 2: Entertainment That I Have Enjoyed
Volume 3: East Coast Trips
Volume 4: Olympics Have Always Intrigued Me
Volume 5: Wonders of the World
Volume 6: Caribbean Cruises We Have Enjoyed
Volume 7: Animals
Volume 8: Storms and Other Major Disasters in My Lifetime
Volume 9: Wars, Terrorist Attacks and Major Disasters

The Cromwell Family Book

Visit Barbara's website to view all of her books
http://barbararaue.ericraue.com

Port Elgin

In 1854, Benjamin Shantz acquired a sawmill on Mill Creek from George Butchart. Nearby he built a gristmill and within three years a community of 250 people developed around these mills. Stores, hotels and tanneries were built and a village plot for Port Elgin was laid out in 1857. Businessmen Henry Hilker, Samuel Bricker, and John Stafford contributed to the development of the settlement. The original economic development of Port Elgin during the 19th century was based on its harbour facilities on Lake Huron constructed in 1857-1858 making the village a distribution centre for the surrounding agricultural region. The arrival of the Wellington, Grey and Bruce Railway in 1872 further stimulated the growth of the community.

Hepworth

Hepworth is located at the base of the Bruce Peninsula, on Highway 6 east of Sauble Beach.

Sauble Beach

Sauble Beach is a resort community on the eastern shore of Lake Huron. The beach is seven miles long.

Shallow Lake

Shallow Lake is located on Highway 6 south and east of Hepworth.

Port Elgin

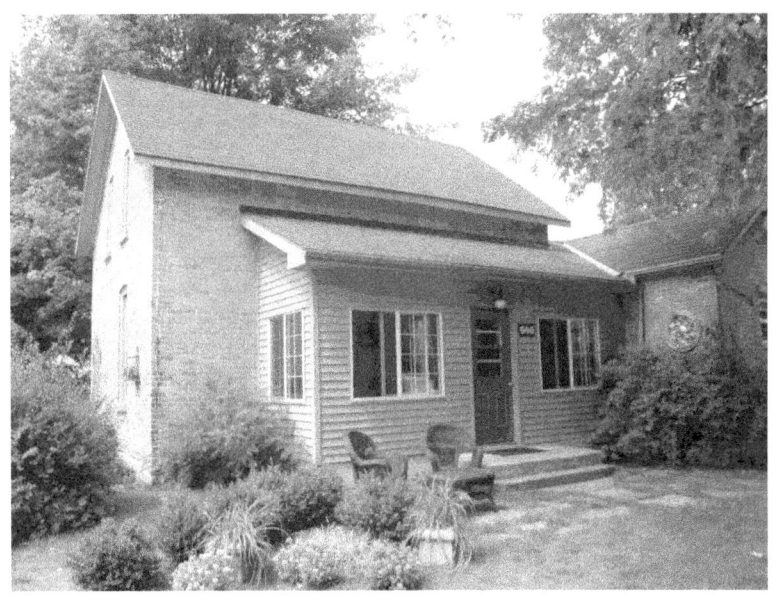

646 Shantz Street - 1½ storey yellow brick – Gothic
Mary and John Zant - 1899

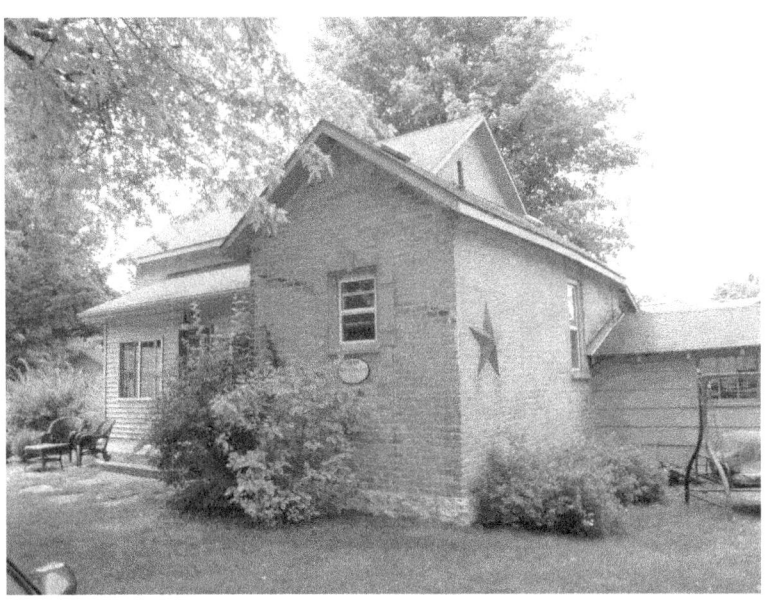

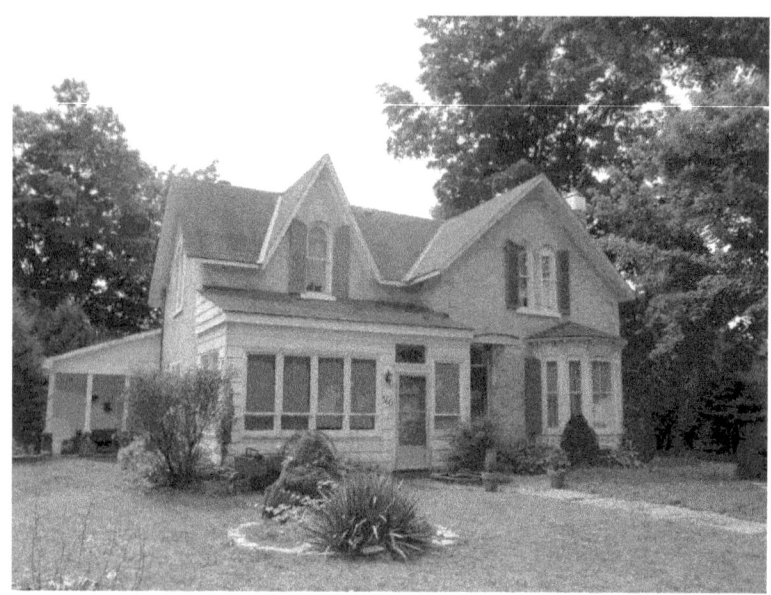

#360 Shantz Street – yellow brick – Gothic Revival

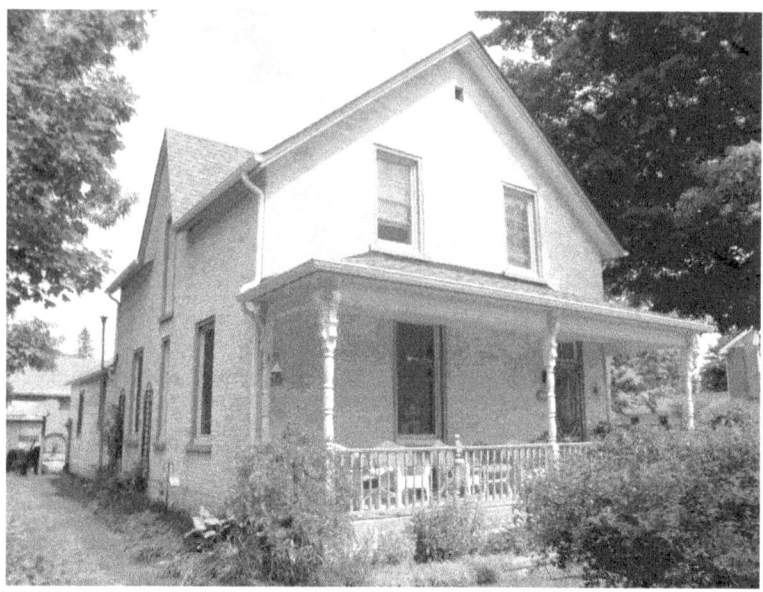

399 Green Street – 1½ storey yellow brick – Gothic style

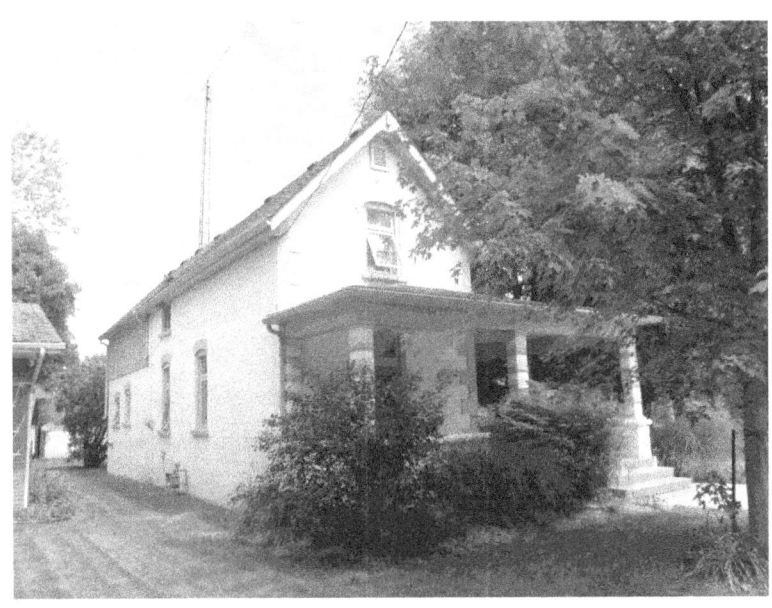

387 Green Street - Harvey J. Gonder, Farm Agent – circa 1895

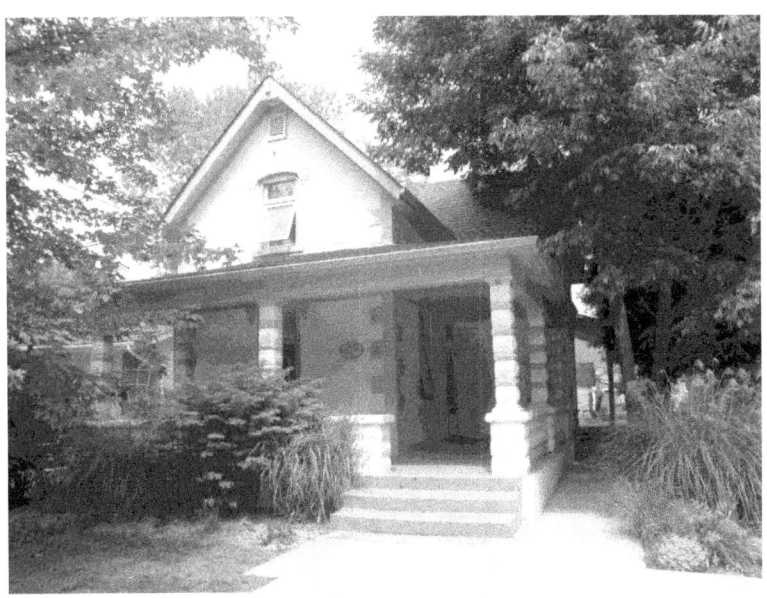

Gothic Revival

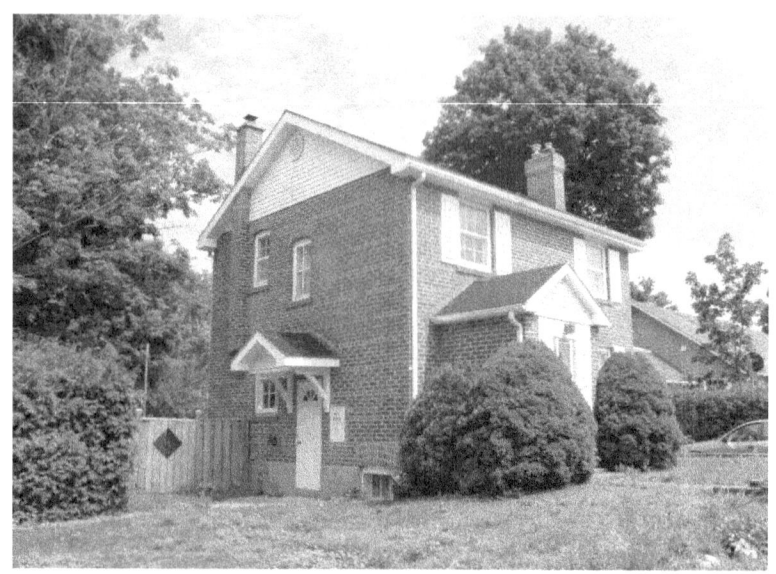

411 Green Street – red brick – two storey

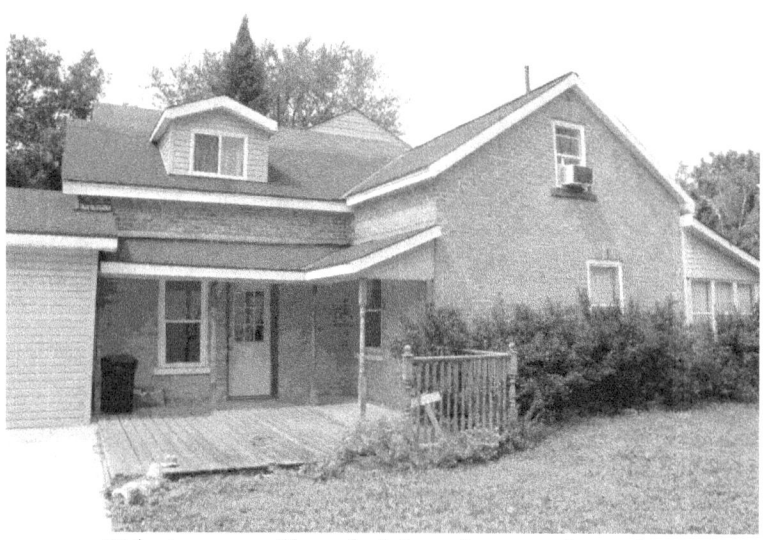

1½ storey yellow brick – dormer in attic

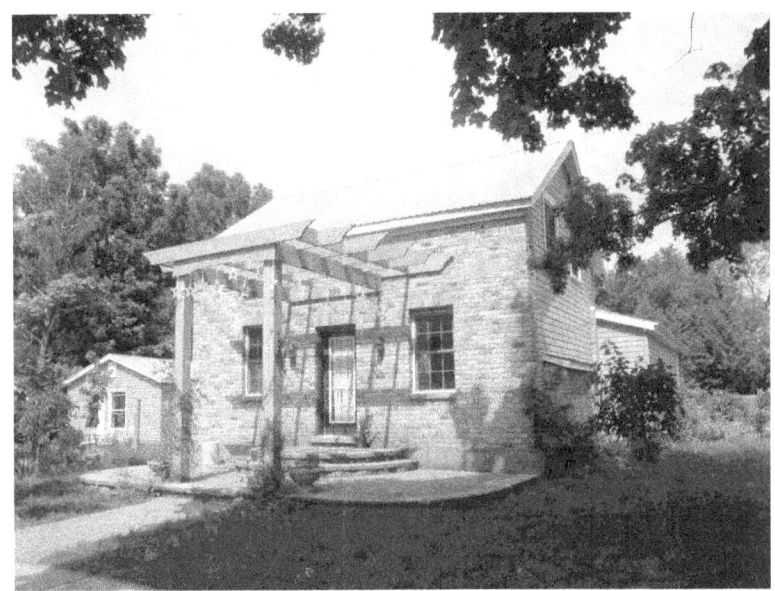

#399 – yellow brick – arbour similar to one Harry built at our townhouse at 100 Quigley Road, Hamilton

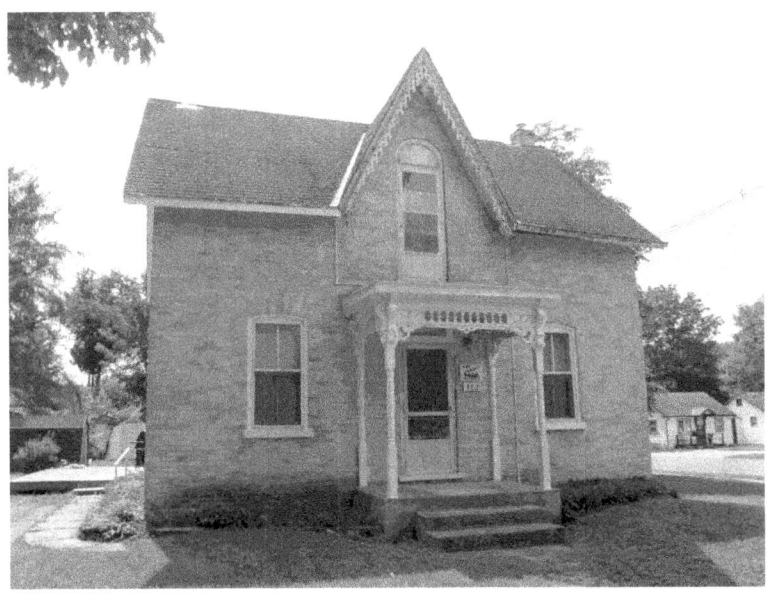

#412 – Gothic Cottage – 1½ storey yellow brick, decorative Vergeboard trim on gable

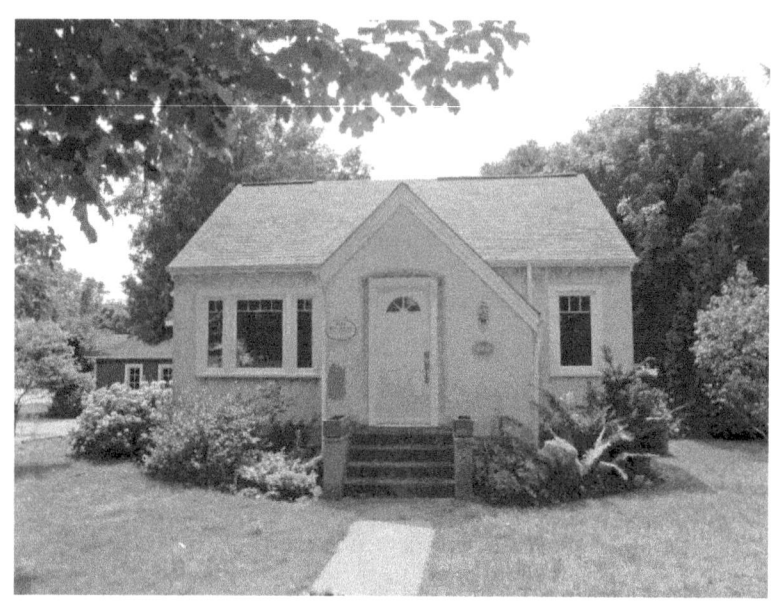

#440 – J. V. Nelles, Medical Doctor – 1945
Stucco exterior

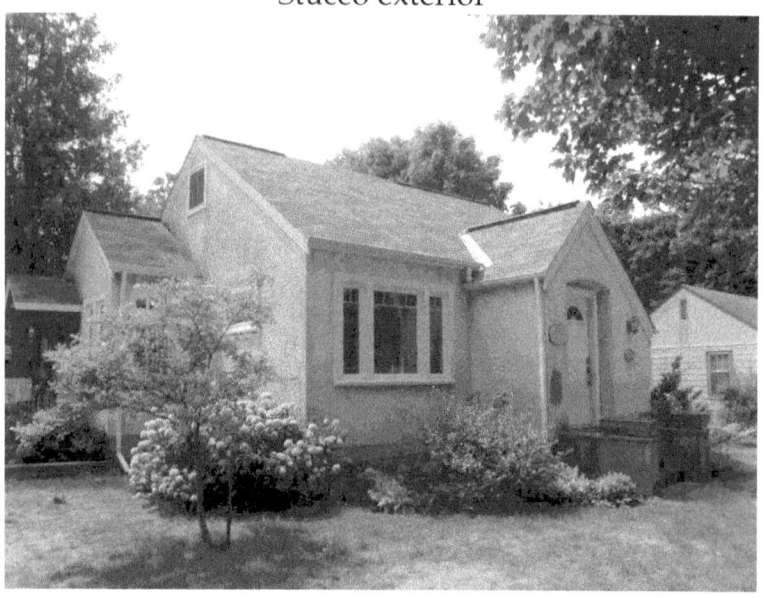

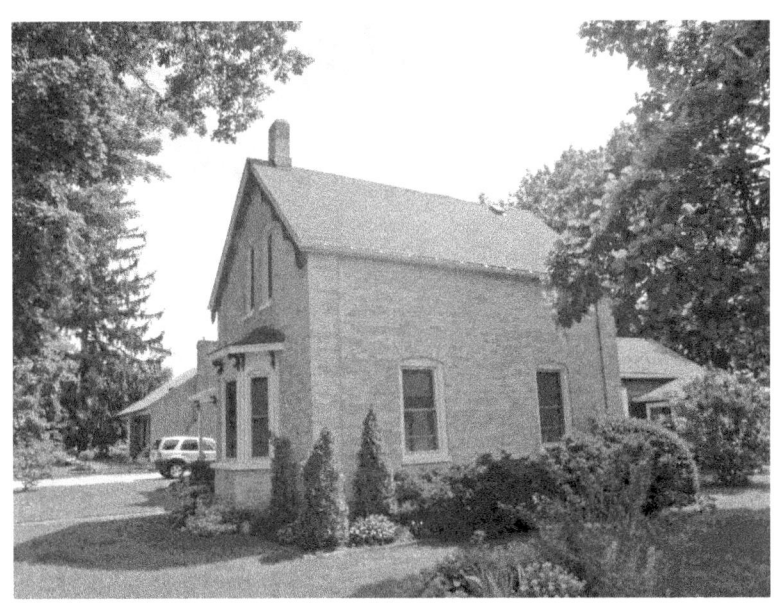

452 Green Street – yellow brick – Gothic Revival – Vergeboard trim, bay window

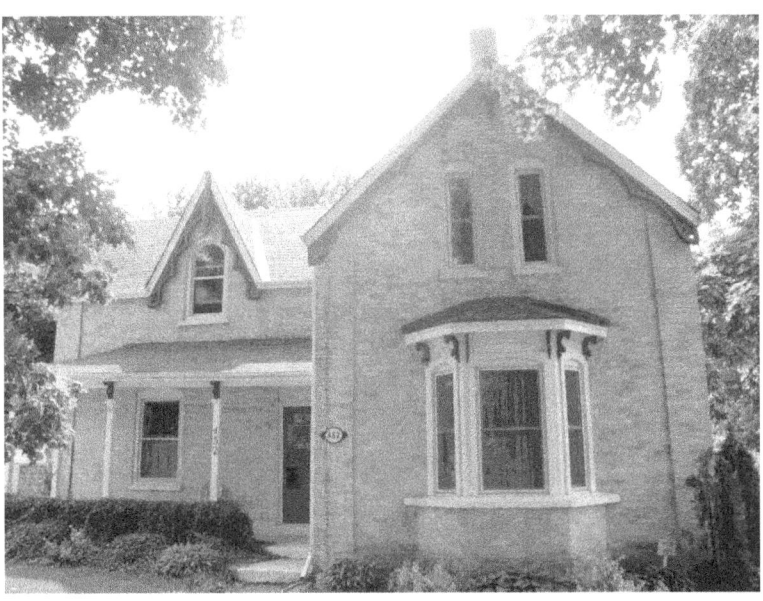

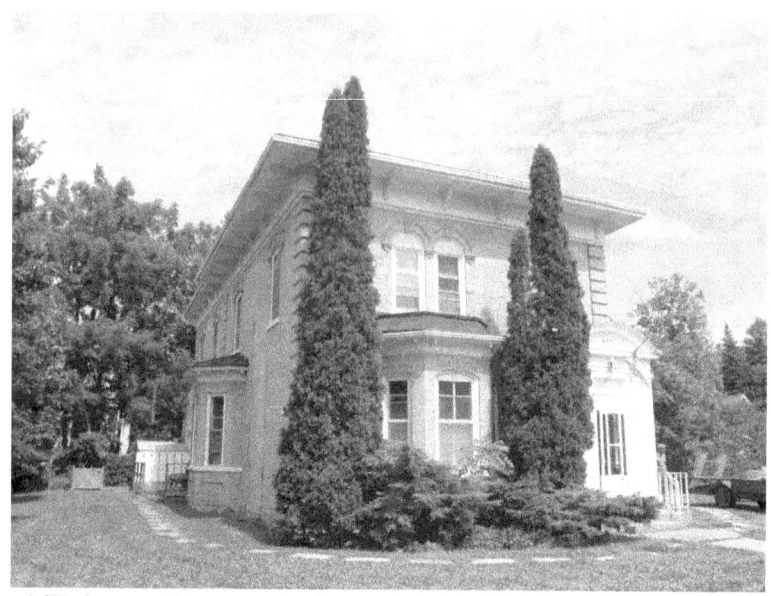
467 Green Street – Italianate style – "Lavrock House"

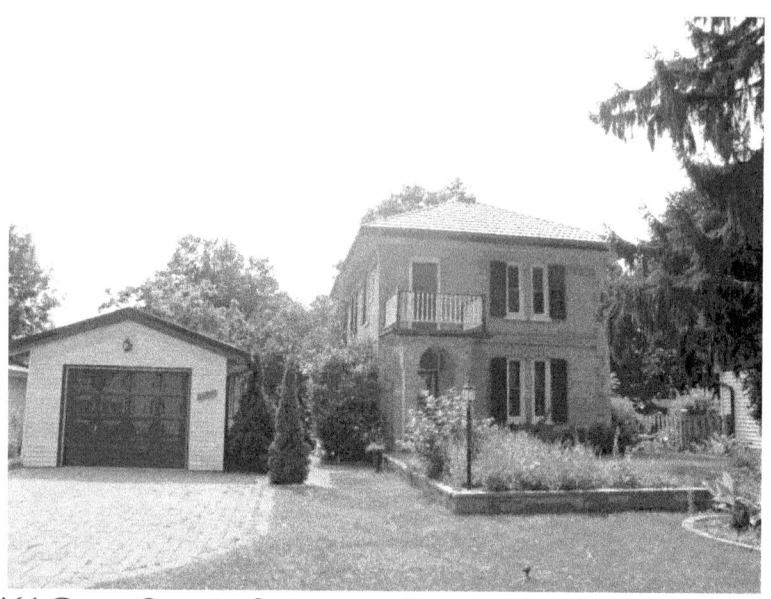
464 Green Street – 2 storey yellow brick – Italianate style

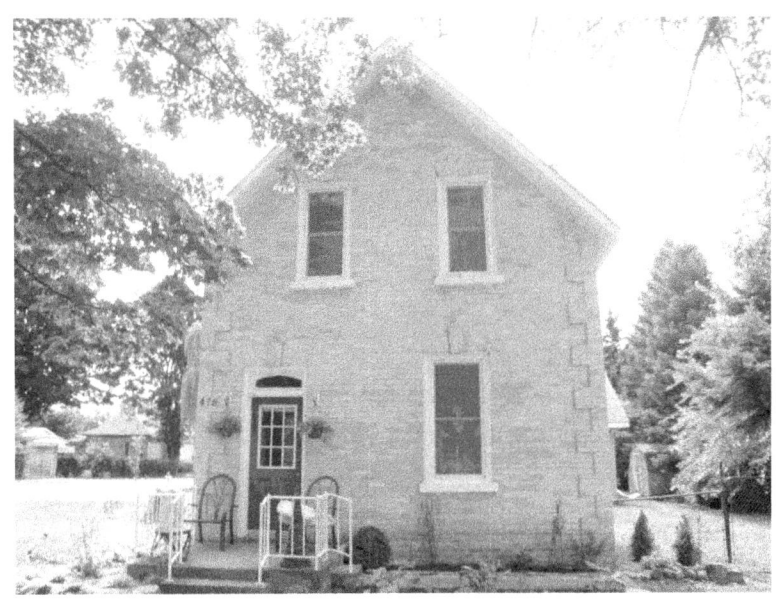

478 Green Street – 1½ storey yellow brick – Gothic Revival
Quoining on corners

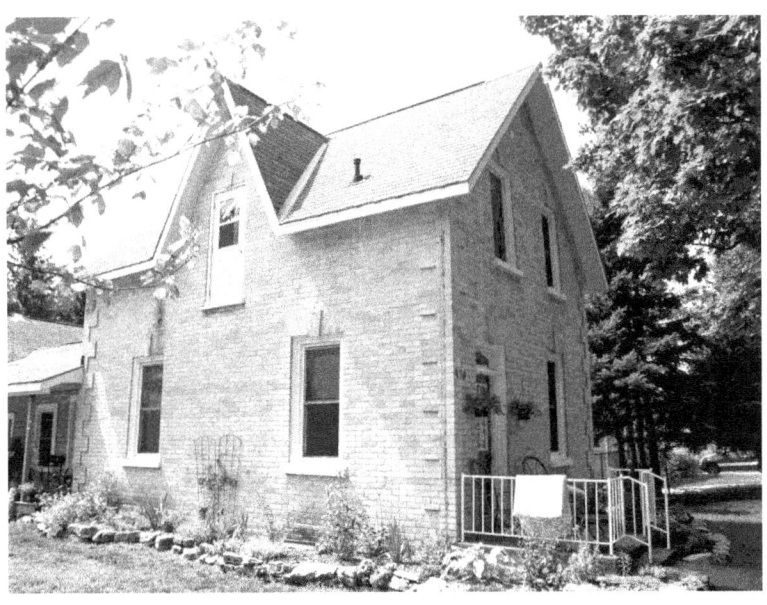

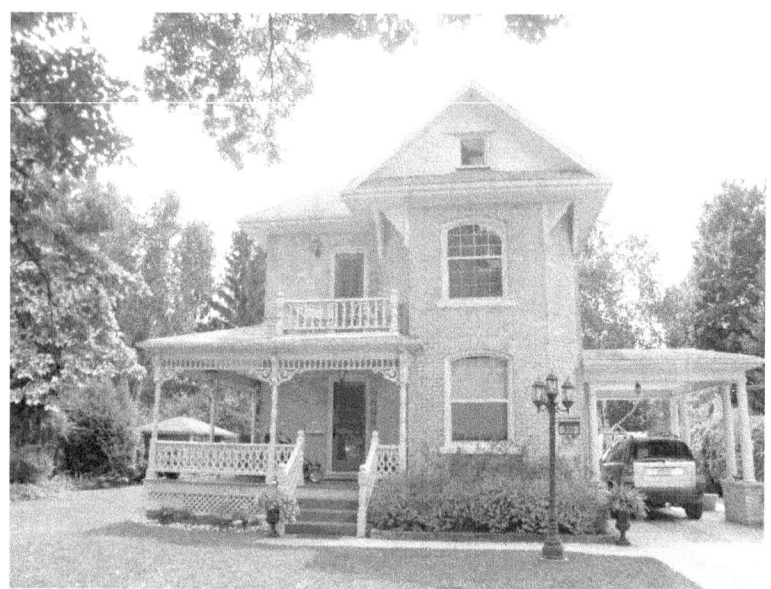

500 Green Street - two-and-a-half storey tower-like bay with projecting eaves and large fretwork pieces resembling brackets.

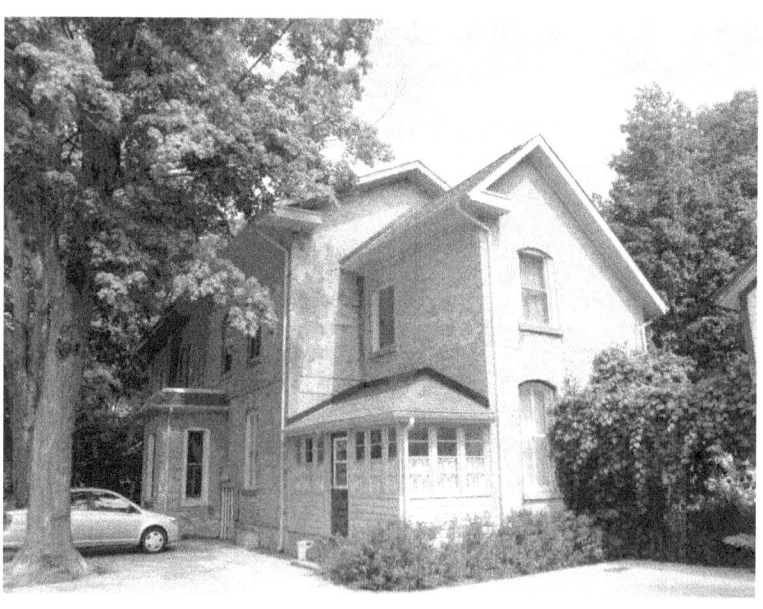

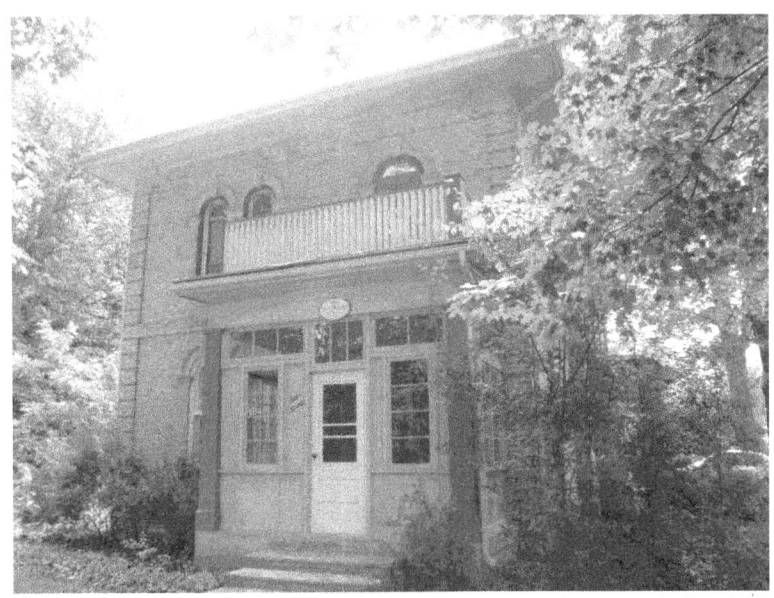

490 Green Street – Hugh McLaren, Merchant - A.D. 1883
2 storey – Italianate style – decorative voussoirs and keystones above windows

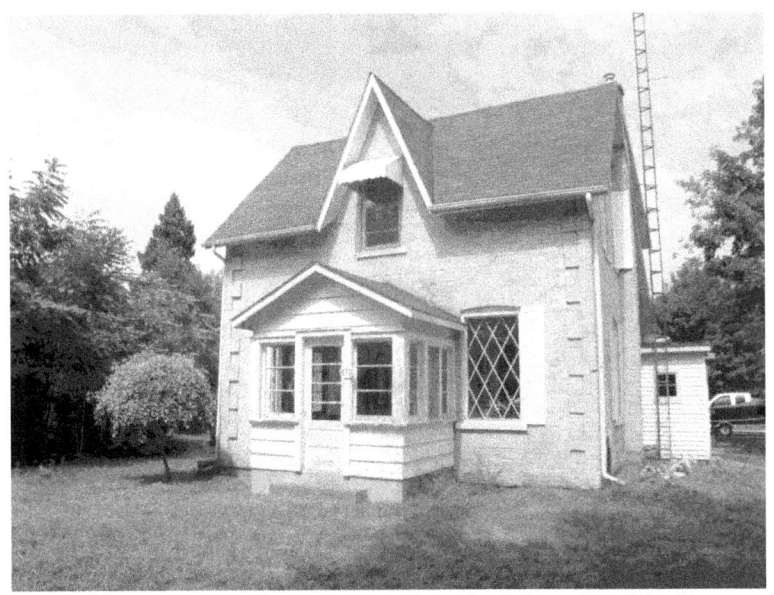

479 Mill Street – 1½ storey yellow brick – Gothic Cottage

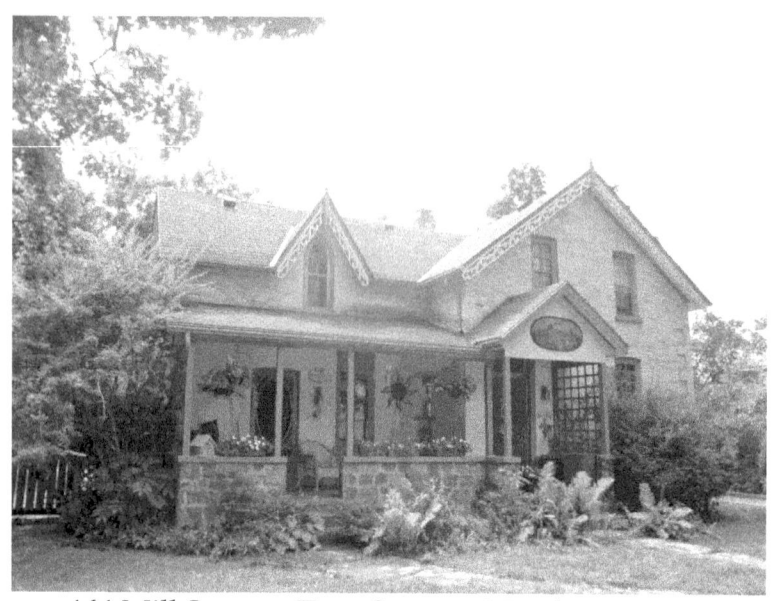

464 Mill Street – Ezra Swartz, Merchant – 1900
Gothic Revival – Vergeboard trim, cobblestone verandah

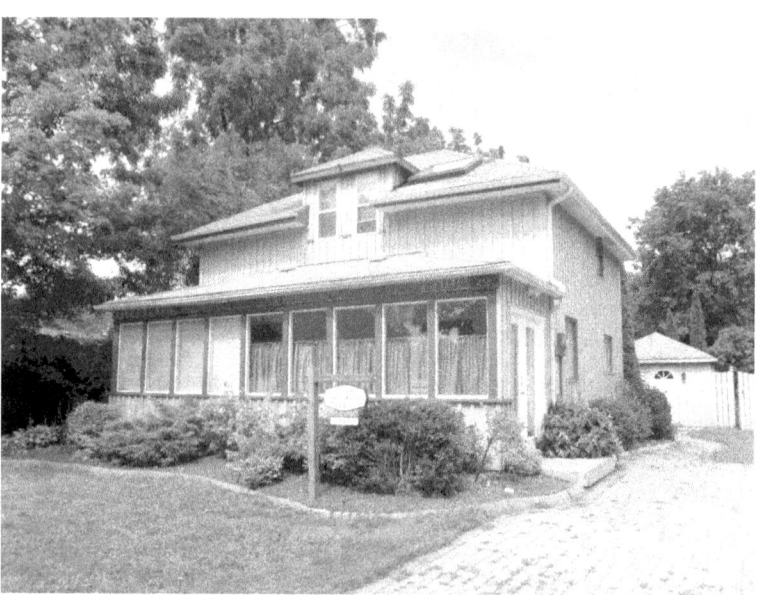

459 Mill Street – Saugeen Hacienda – Italianate style, dormer in attic

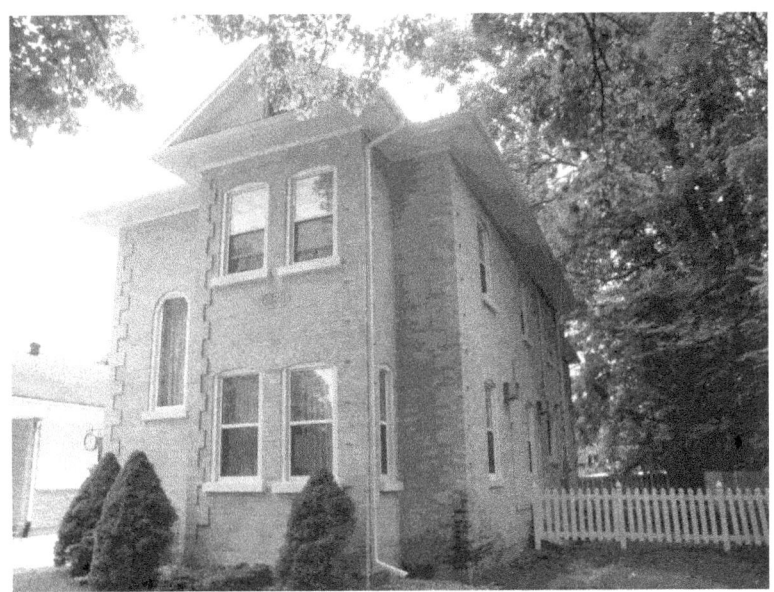

Italianate style – 1888 – yellow brick with two-storey tower capped by a triangular pediment with window

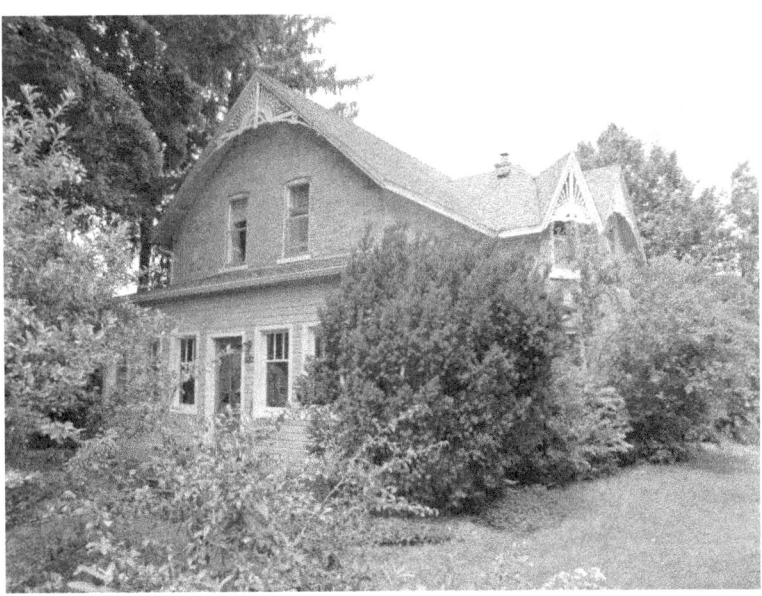

517 Mill Street – yellow brick, Vergeboard trim, Gothic

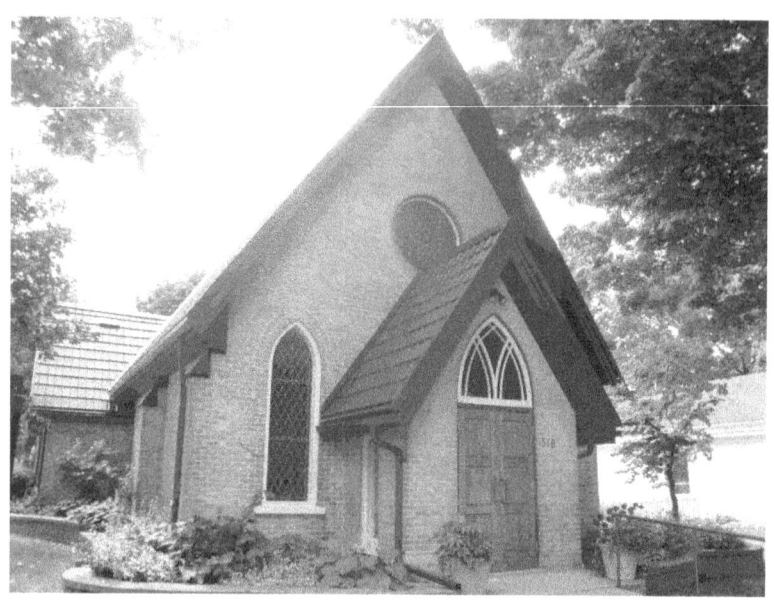

St. John's Anglican Church, 516 Mill Street – rose window, lancet windows

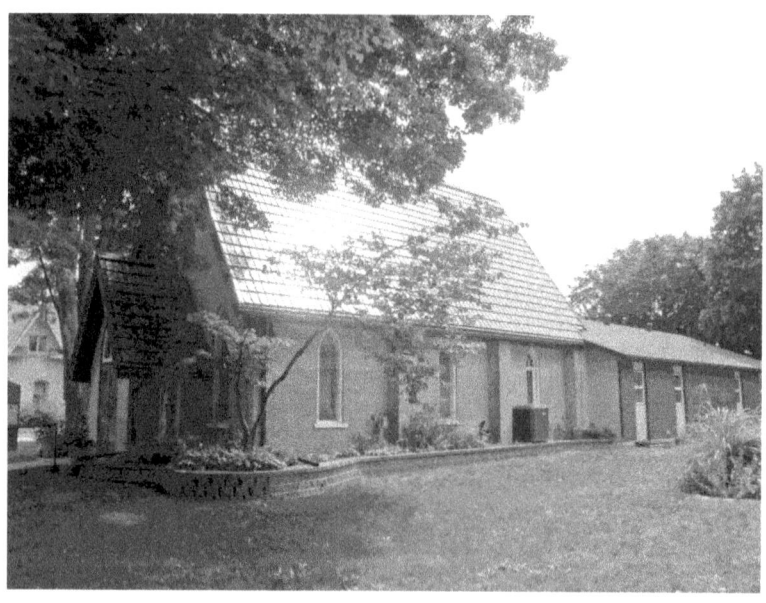

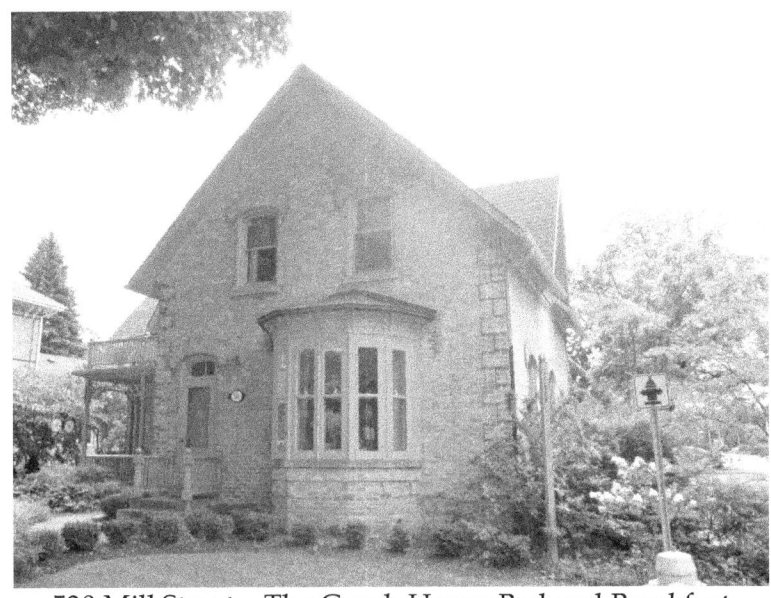

530 Mill Street – The Coach House Bed and Breakfast
Yellow brick, arched voussoirs, cornice brackets on bay window, quoining on corners

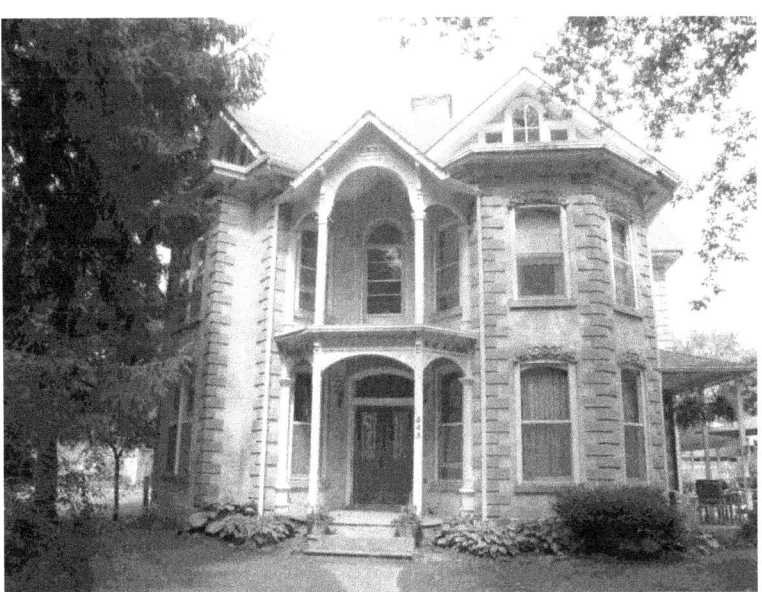

543 Mill Street – Queen Anne style – yellow brick, quoins, Palladian windows in gables, large fretwork pieces resembling brackets on eaves of second floor porch, decorative window hoods

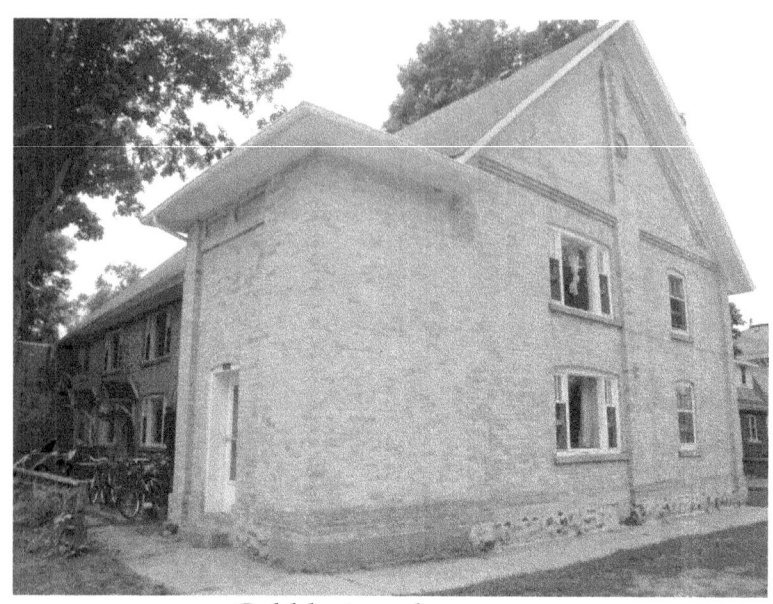

Cobblestone basement
C. M. Church erected A.D. 1871

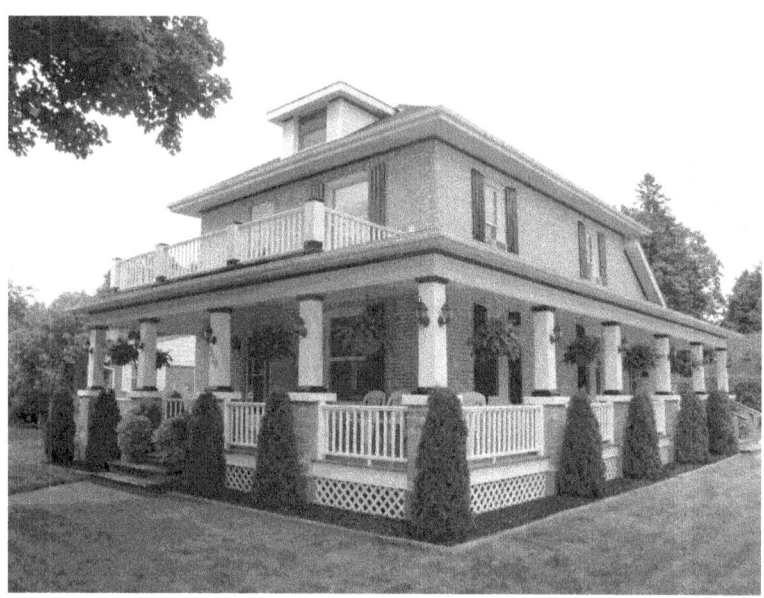

559 Mill Street – Italianate style, wrap-around porch, second floor balcony, dormer in attic – Henry Ebert, Merchant - 1923

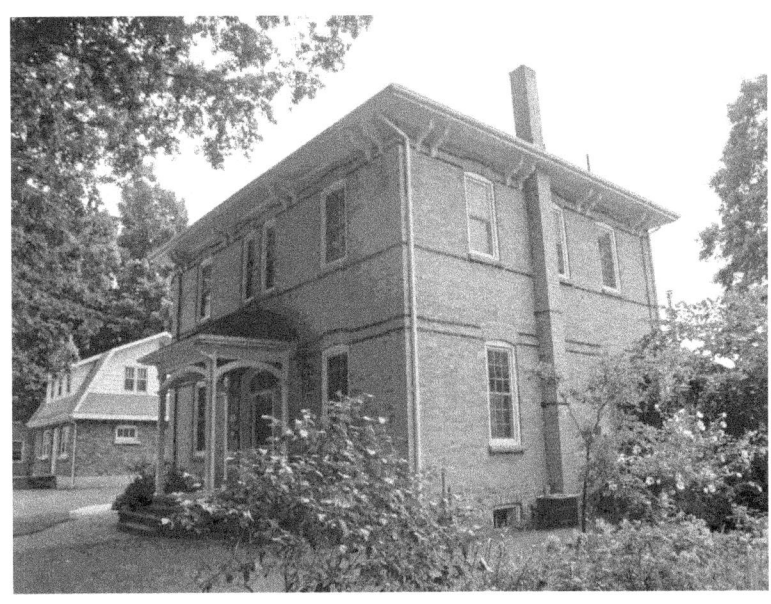

536 Mill Street – yellow brick, Italianate style – paired cornice brackets, dichromatic banding, bay window

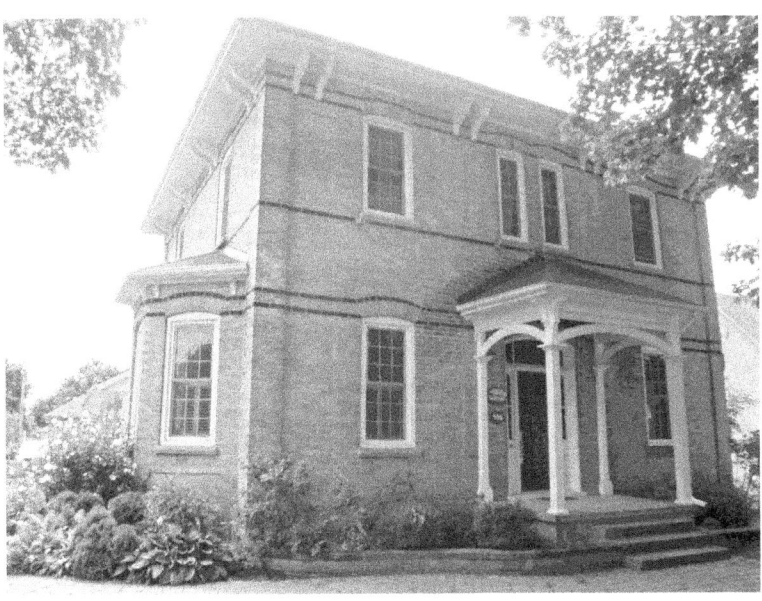

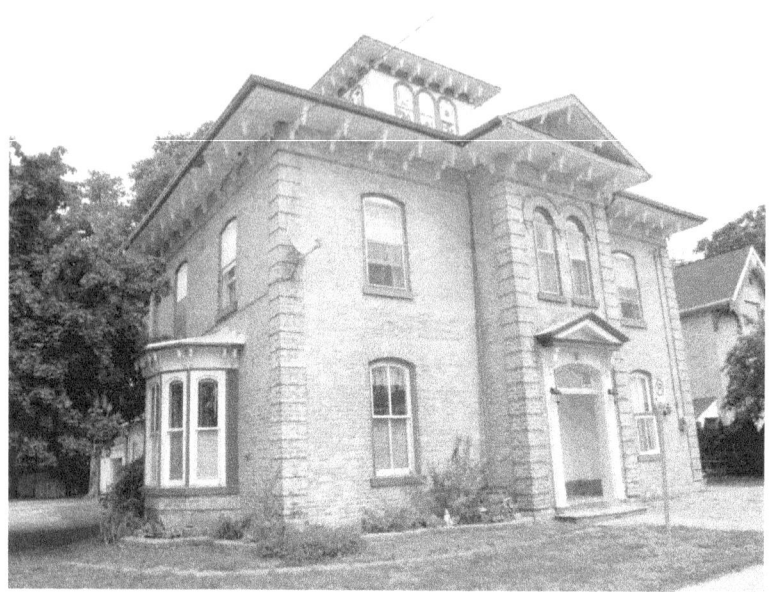

Italianate with belvedere on roof, two storey frontispiece with triangular pediment and arched window hoods, single cornice brackets, bay window

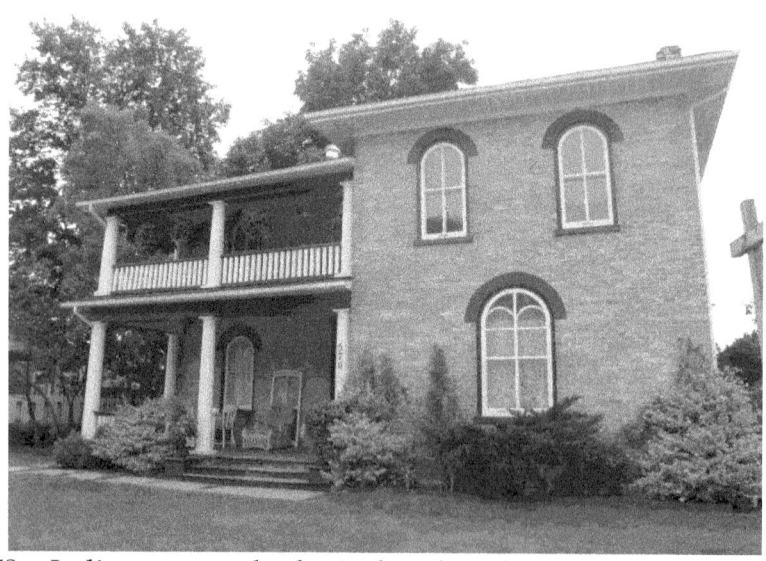

#570 – Italianate – arched window hoods in contrasting colour to yellow brick

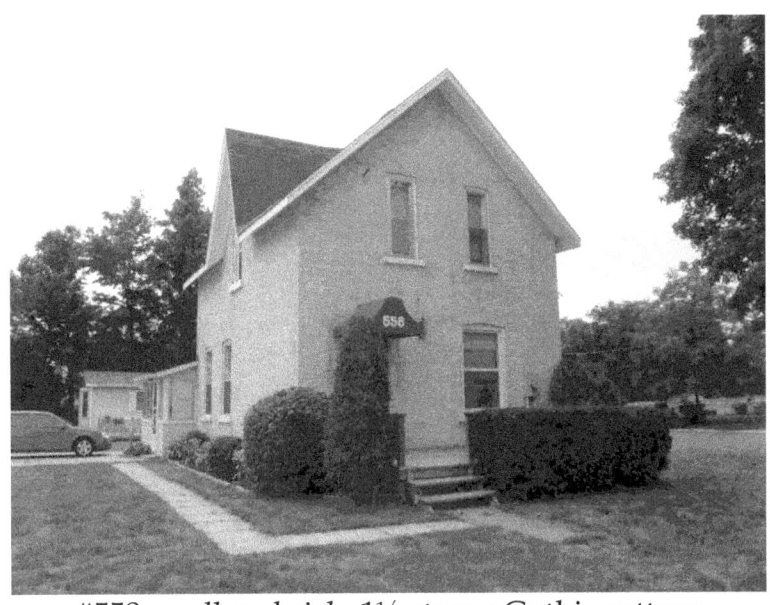

#558 – yellow brick, 1½ storey Gothic cottage

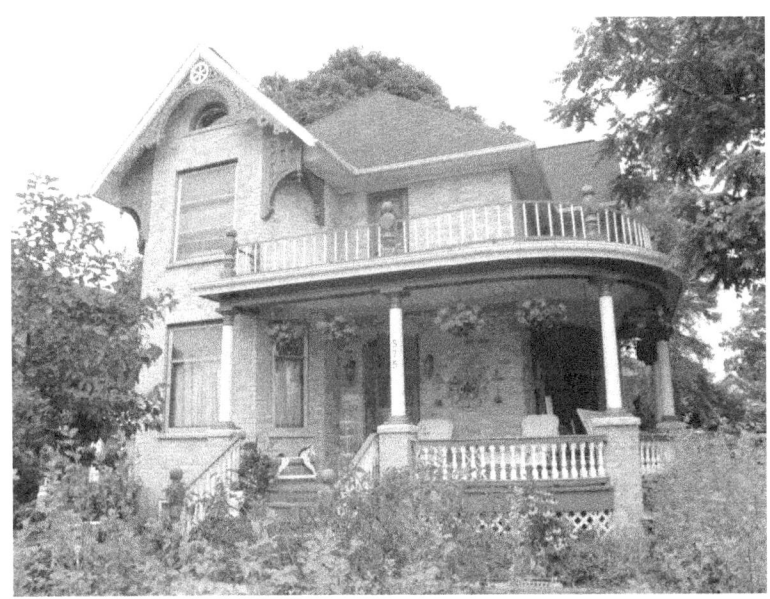

#575 – Italianate style with two-and-a-half storey tower-like bay with projecting eaves and large fretwork pieces resembling brackets, wrap-around verandah on first and second storeys

Downtown

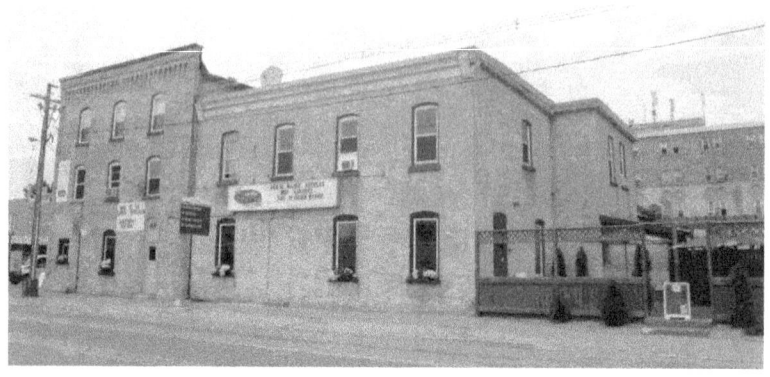

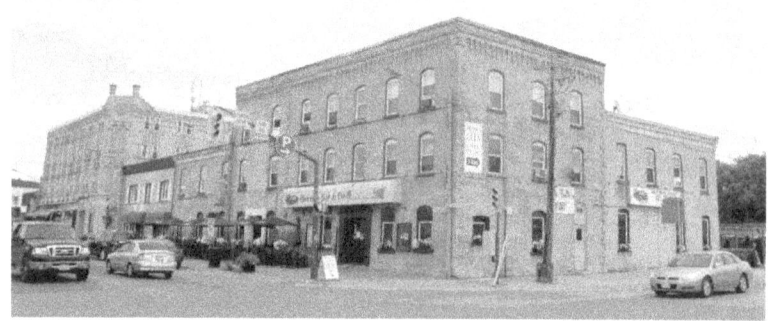

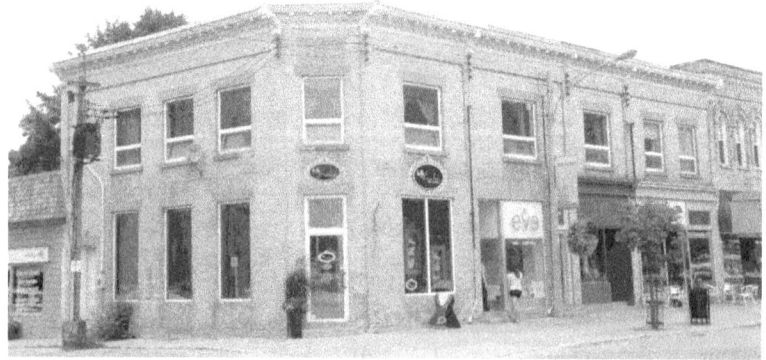

Dentil moulding below cornice brackets

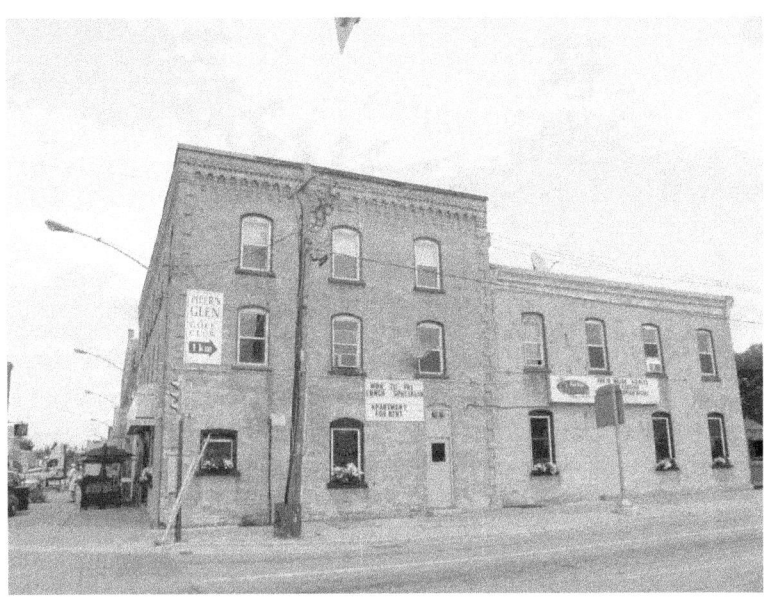

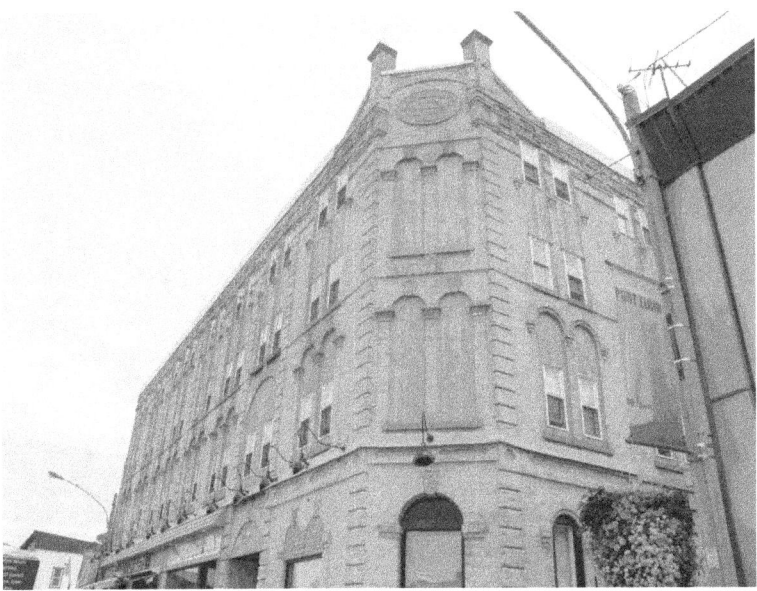

D. O. Bricker and Co's Block, erected 1880, builder D. J. Izzerd

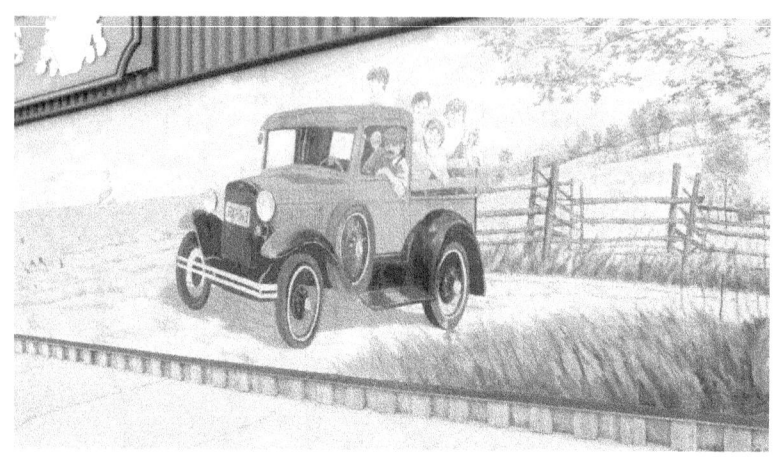

Murals

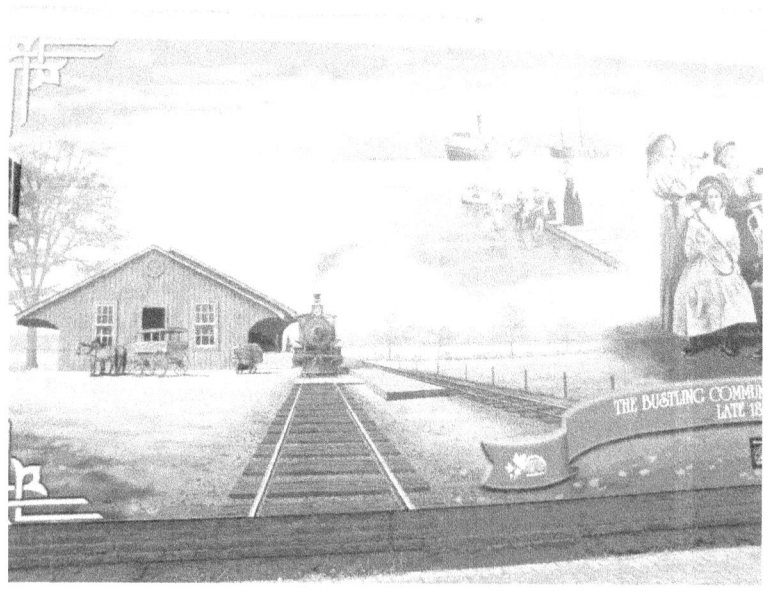

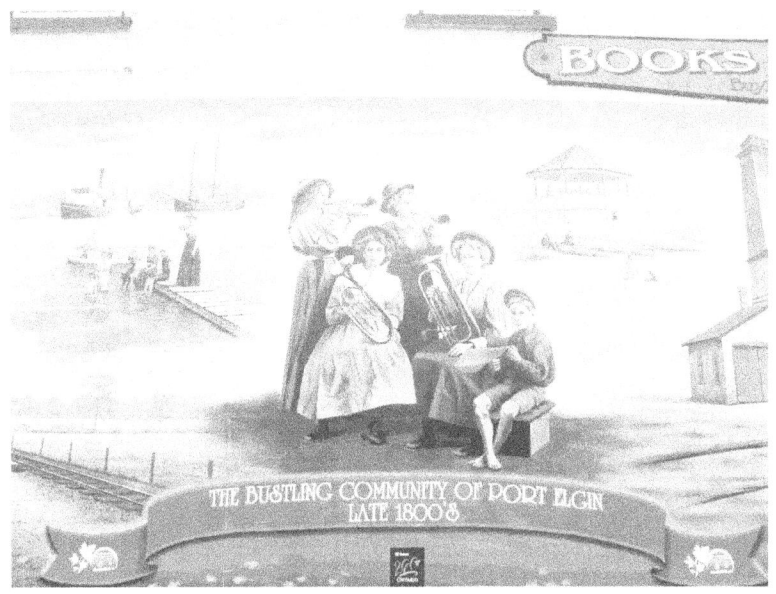

Murals

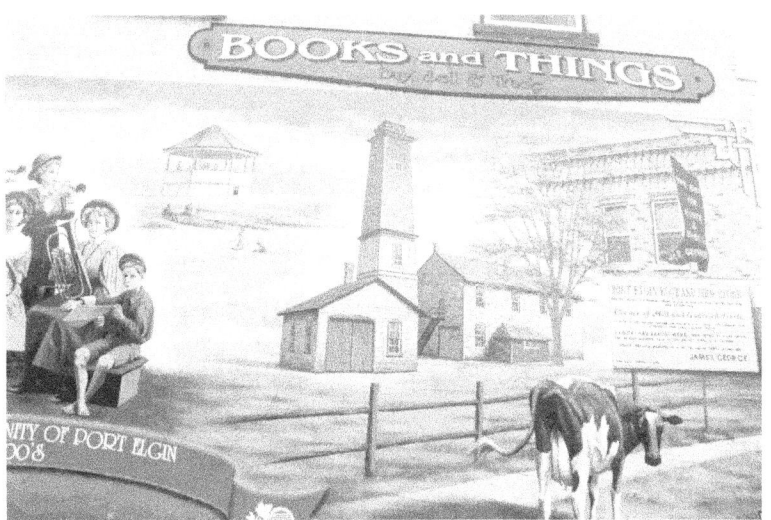

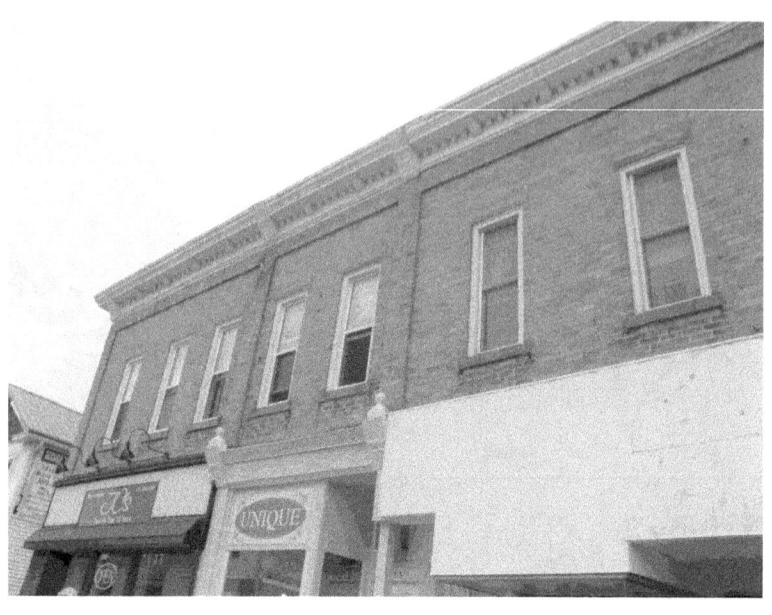

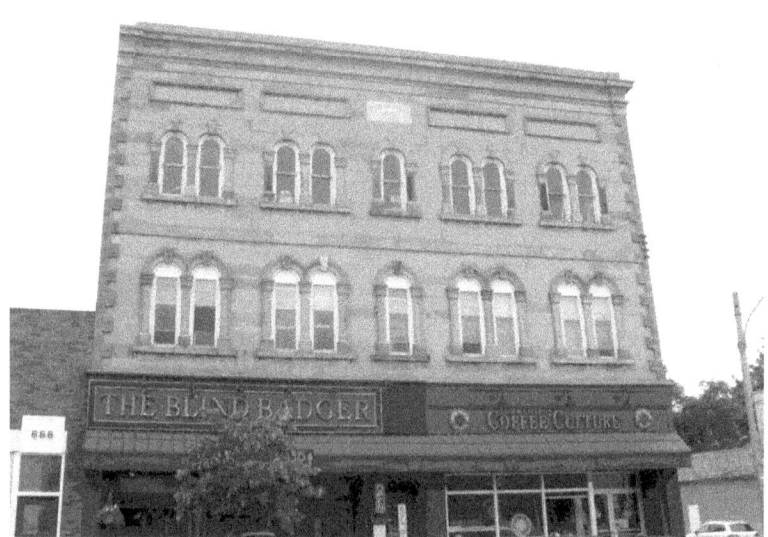

Decorative voussoirs and keystones
Commercial buildings erected A.D. 1878

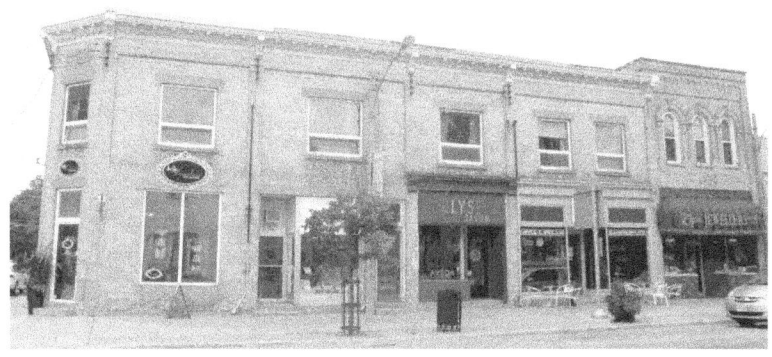

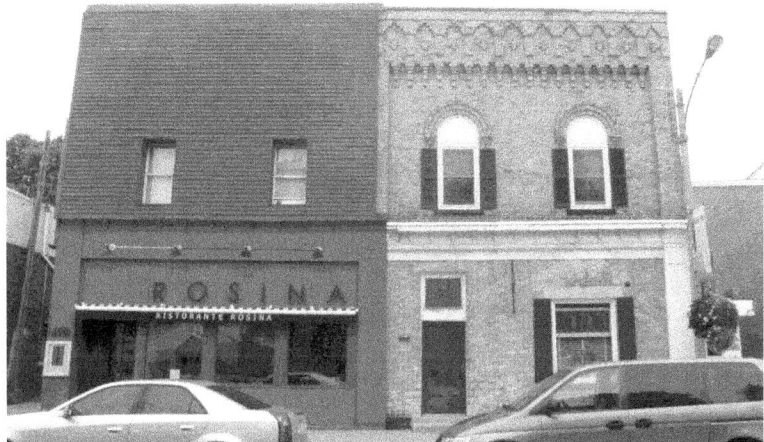

Decorative brickwork, arched window hoods

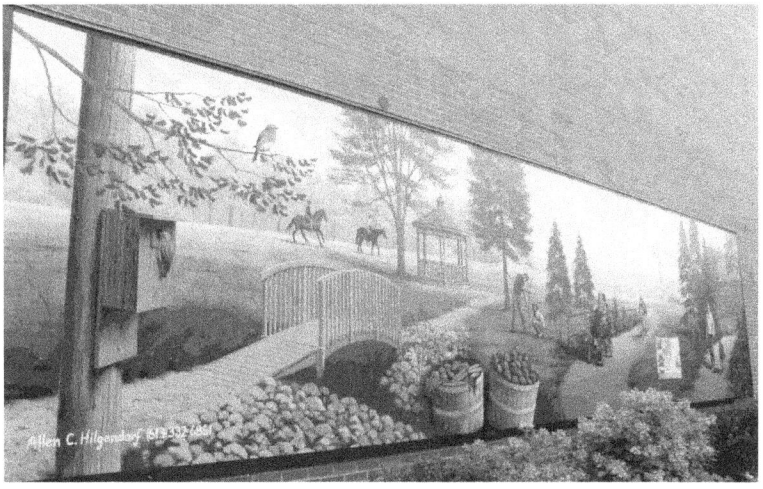

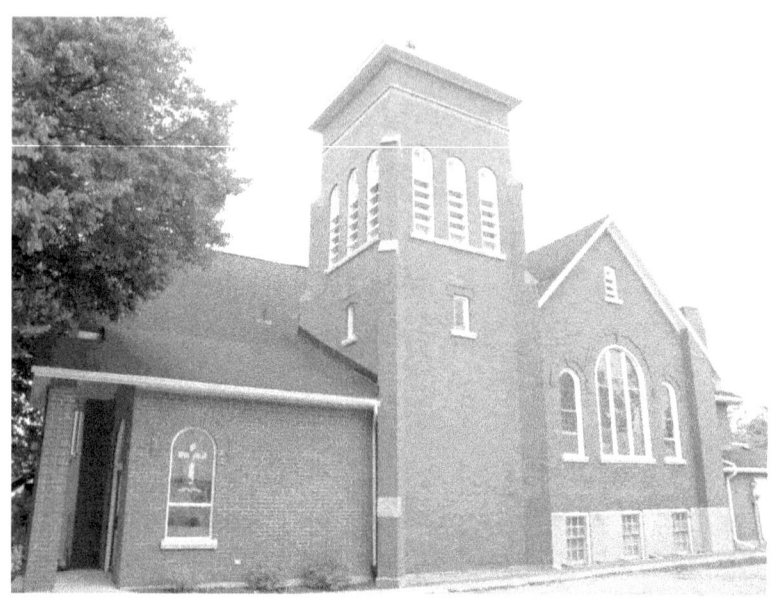

Tolmie Memorial Presbyterian Church erected A.D. 1926
Red brick – Gothic Revival style – lancet windows

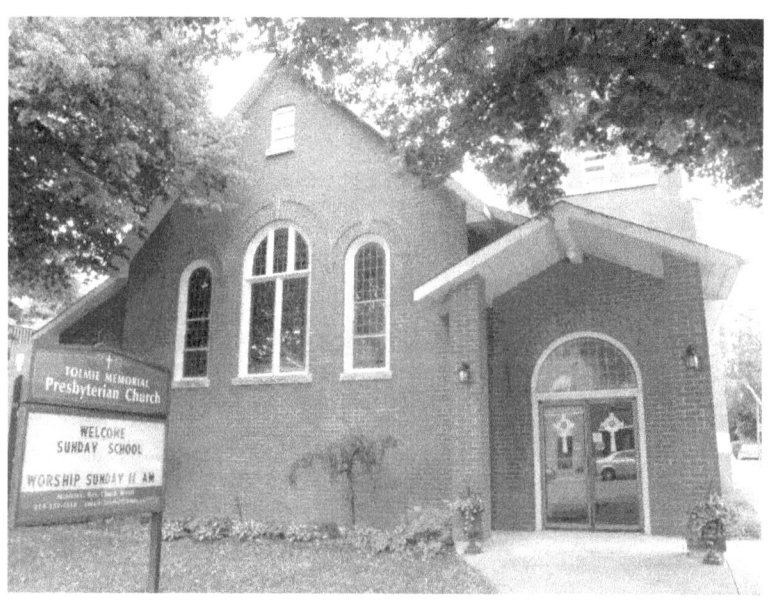

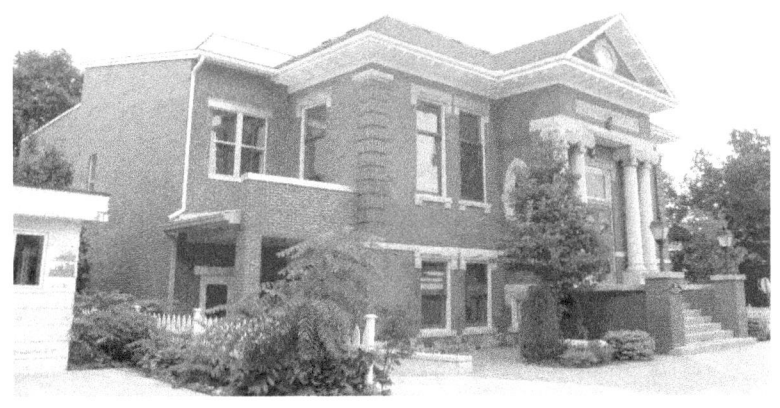

Port Elgin Public Library

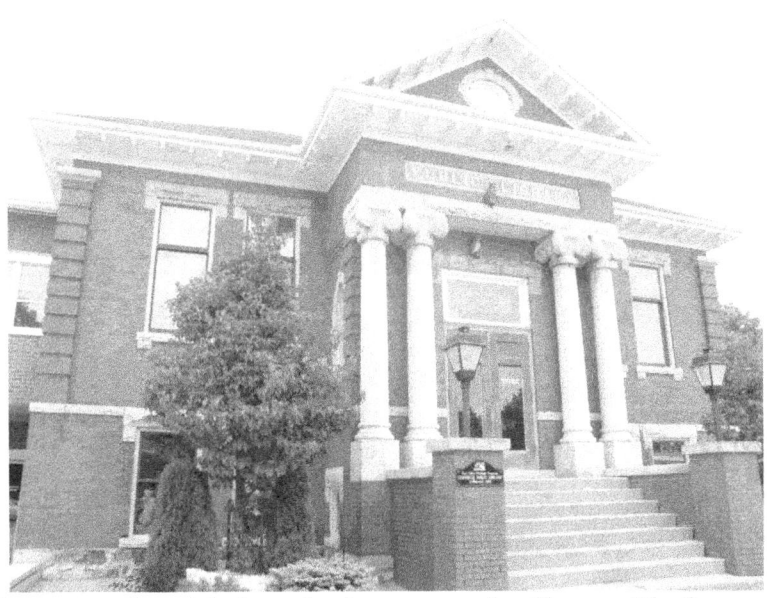

Italianate style with frontispiece, round pillars with decorative capitals, triangular pediment with round window, stone window lintels

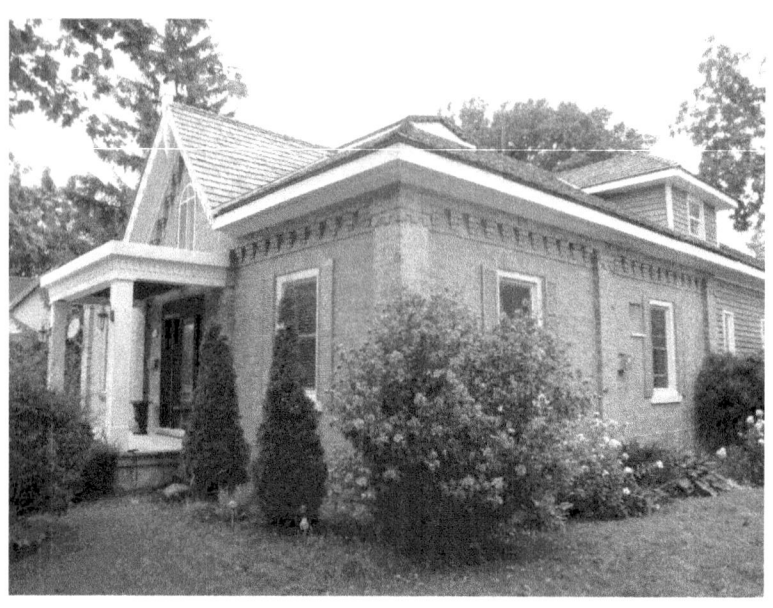

591 Elgin Street – Italianate style with frontispiece, decorative brickwork in tympanum, decorative brickwork below cornice. Finial and trim on gable above front door

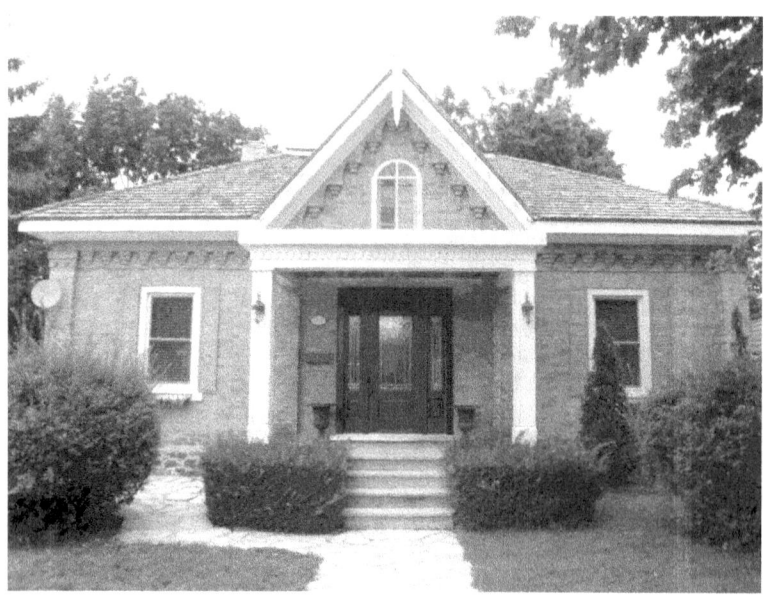

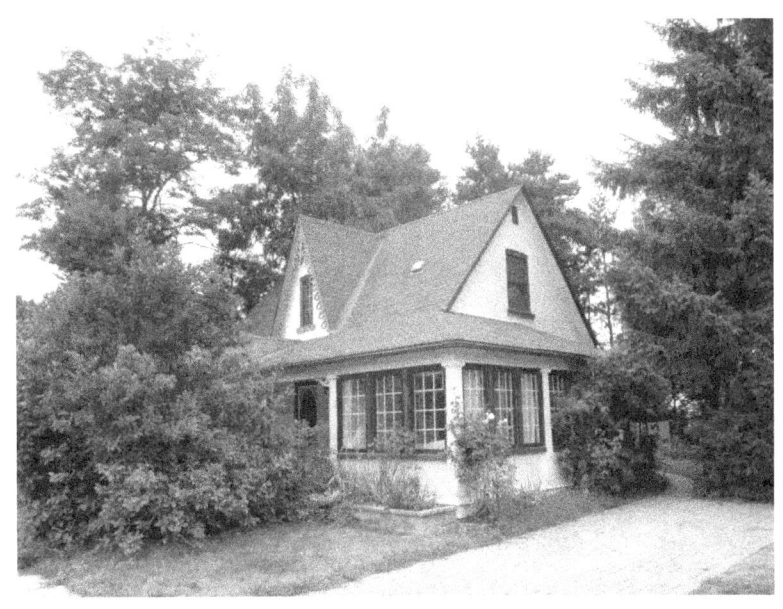

Gothic Cottage – Vergeboard trim on gable

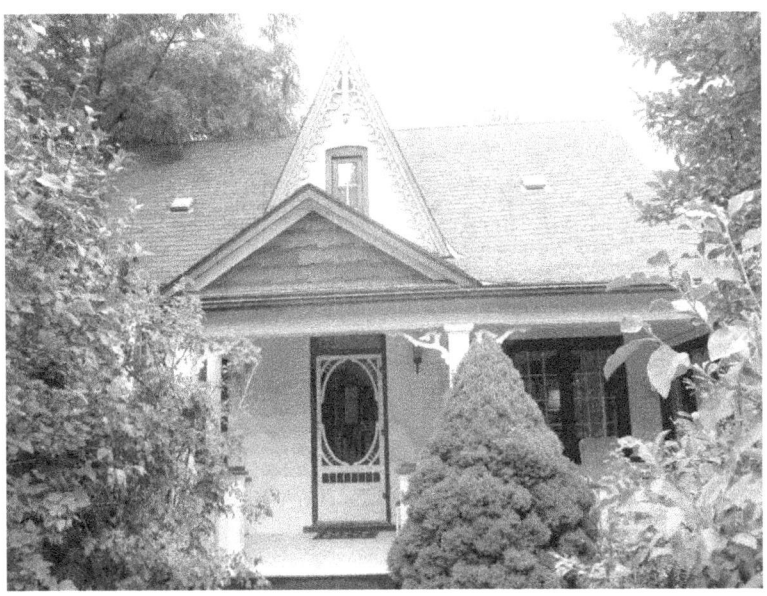

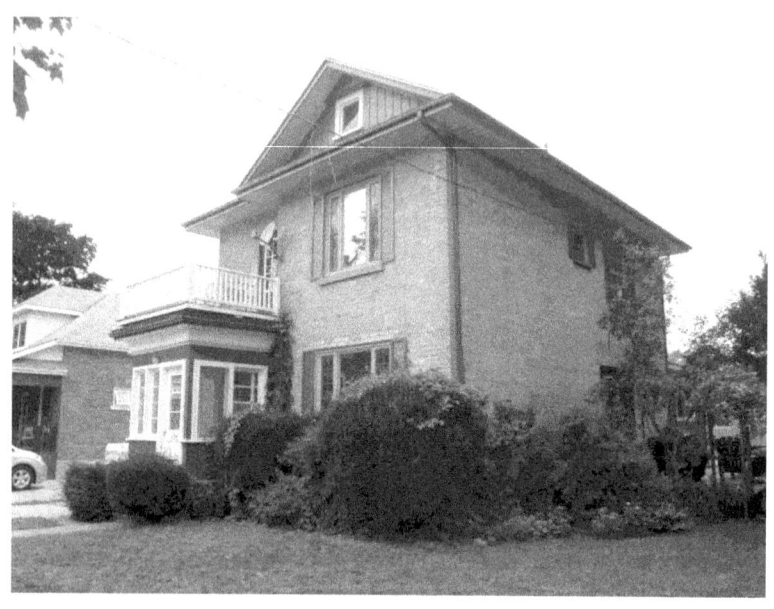

575 Elgin Street - Yellow brick, Italianate style, with gabled dormer in attic

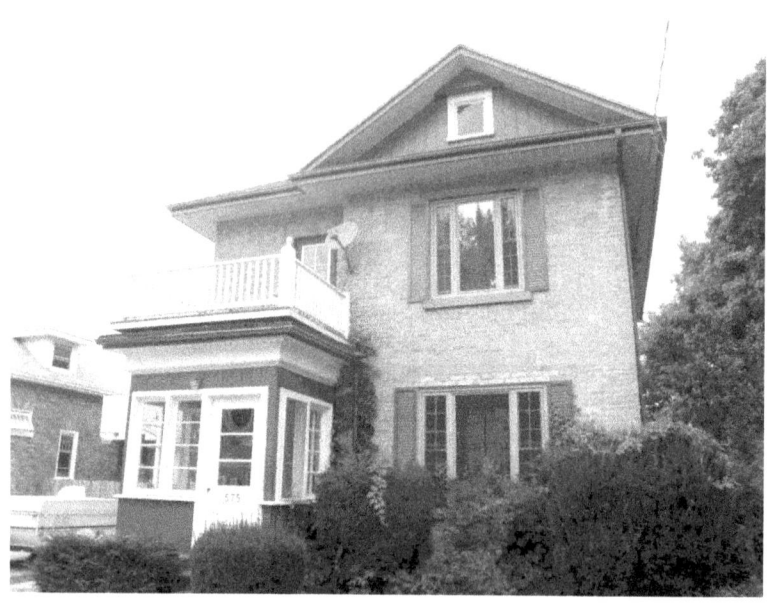

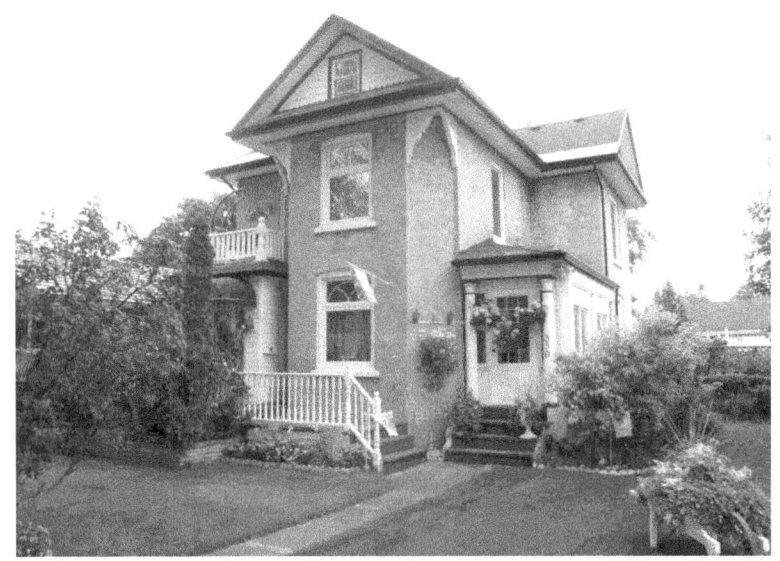

559 Elgin Street - large fretwork pieces resembling brackets under gable – yellow brick which has lots of lime in it

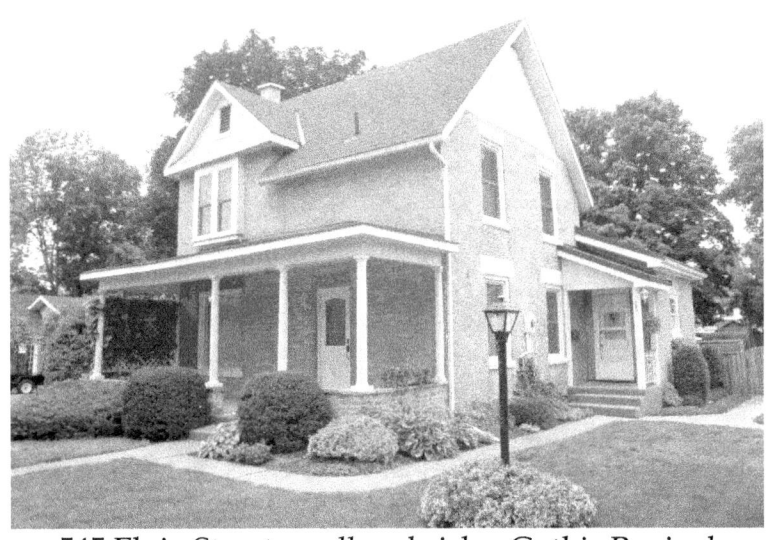

545 Elgin Street – yellow brick – Gothic Revival

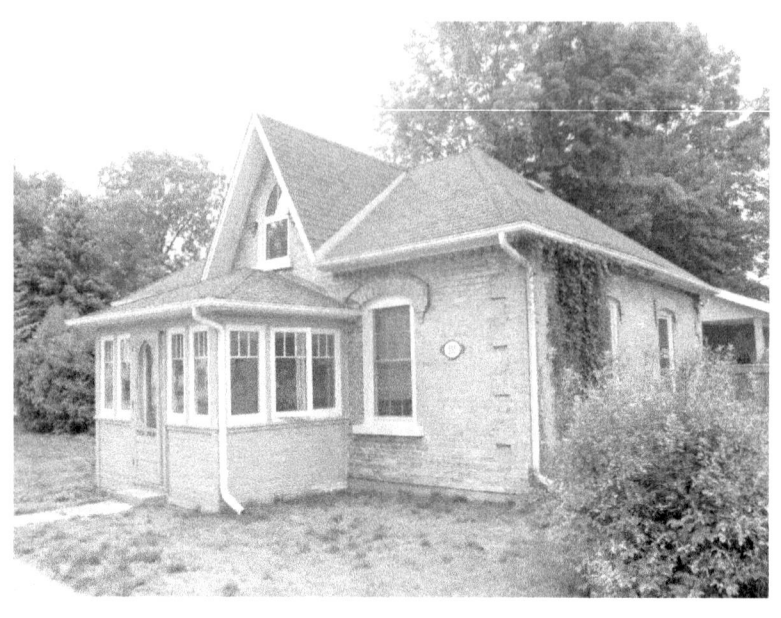

535 Elgin Street – yellow brick one storey Gothic cottage, decorative brick window voussoirs

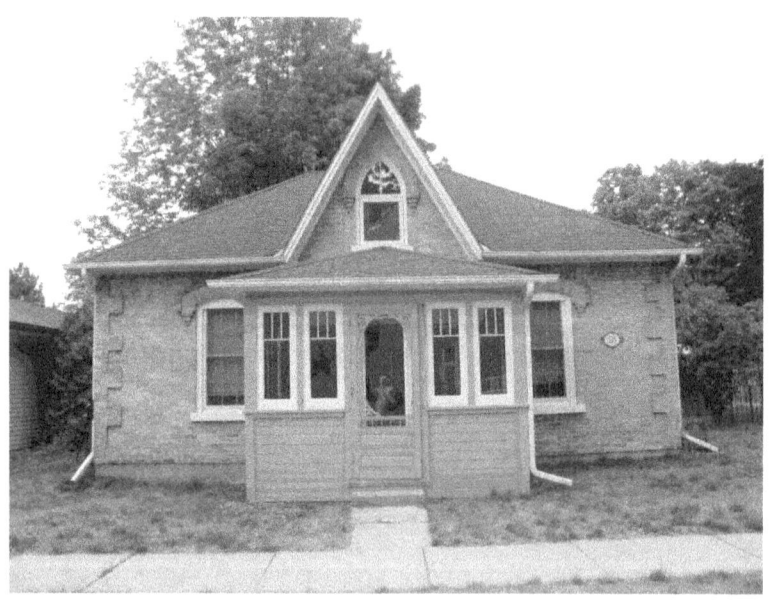

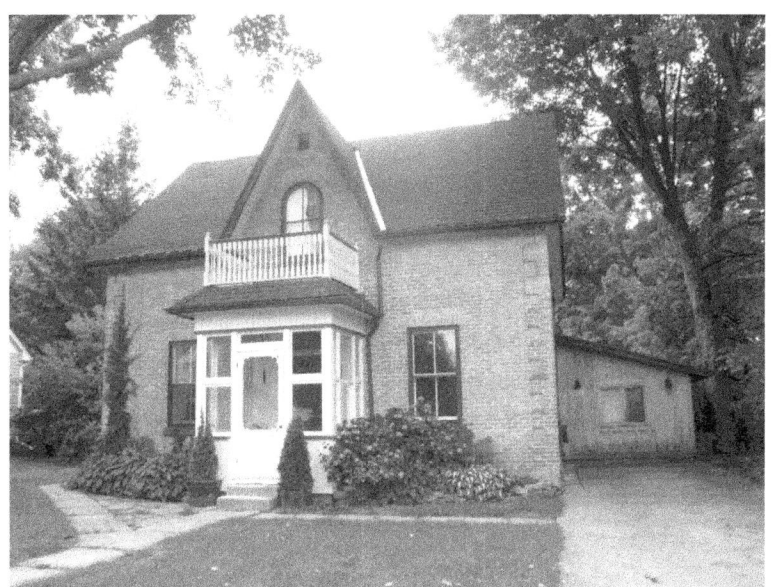

1½ storey Gothic Cottage with balcony off attic dormer

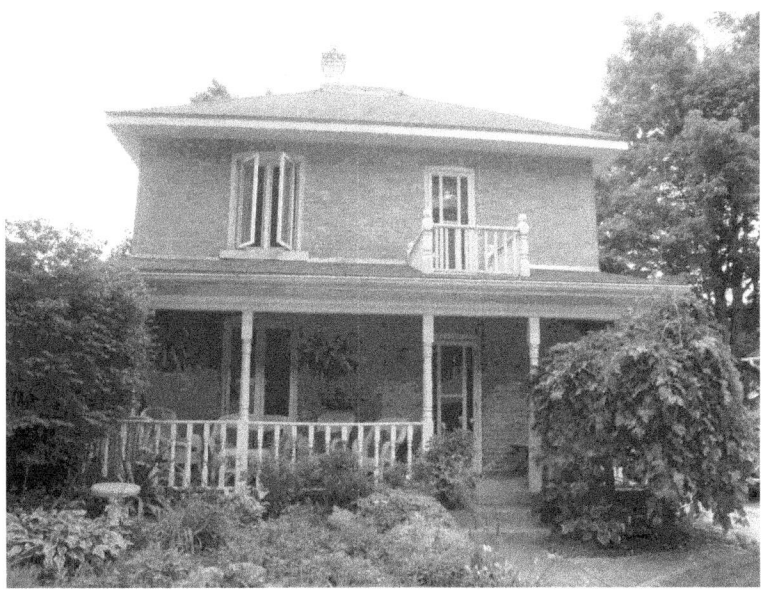

503 Elgin Street – Italianate style, hip roof, two storey

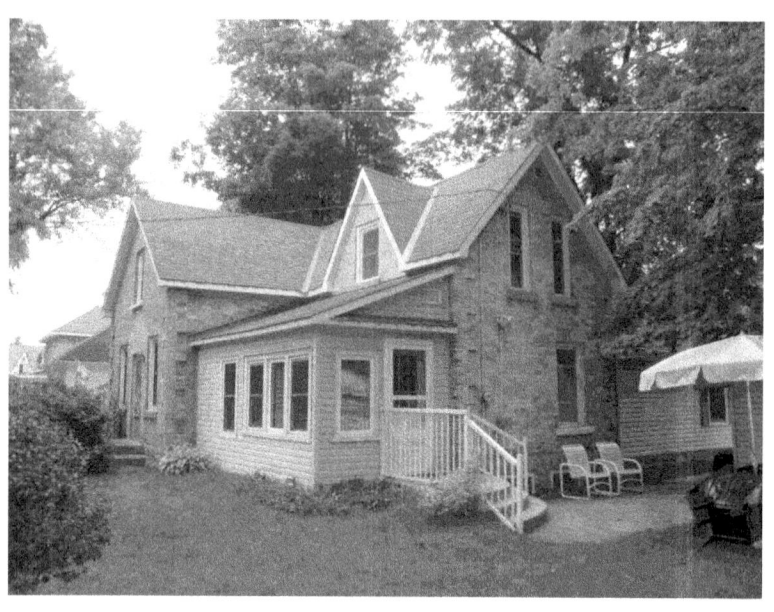

515 Elgin Street – yellow brick, quoins

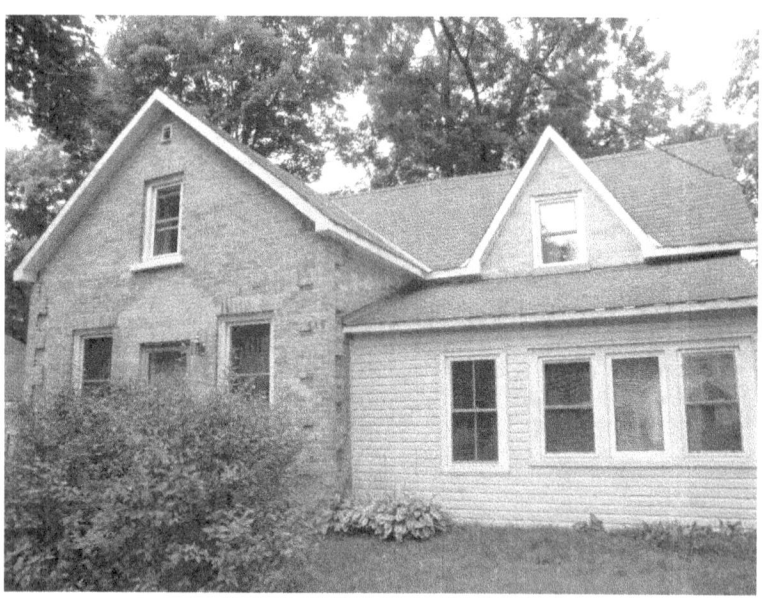

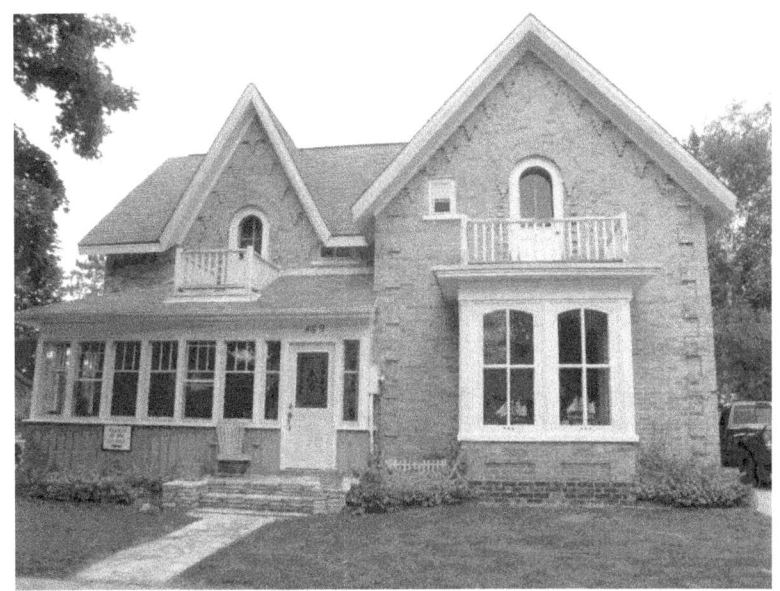

489 Elgin Street – Gothic Revival – decorative brickwork, quoins, balconies off doors in attic gables

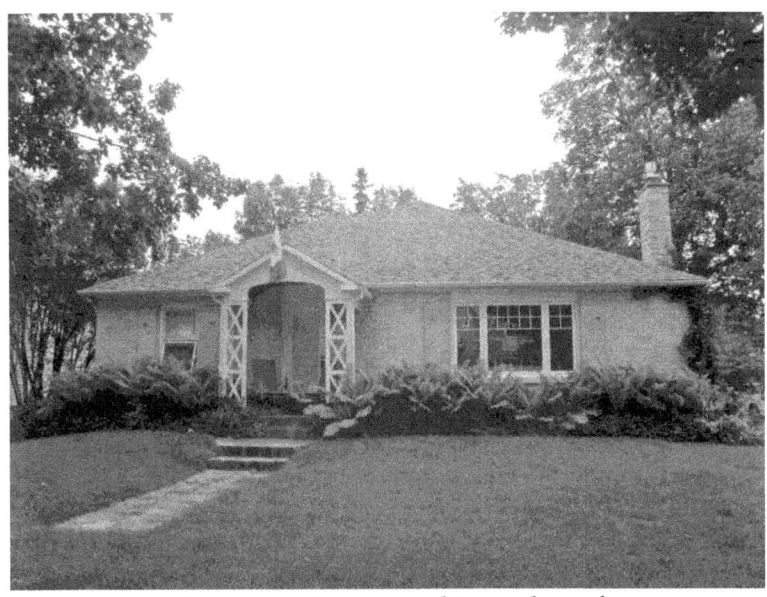

Regency Cottage – hipped roof

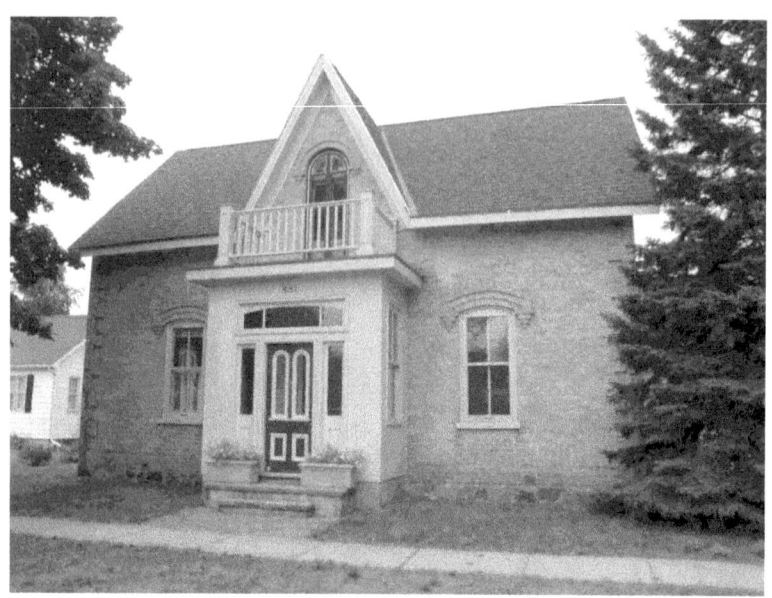

481 Elgin Street – Gothic Cottage – arched window hoods

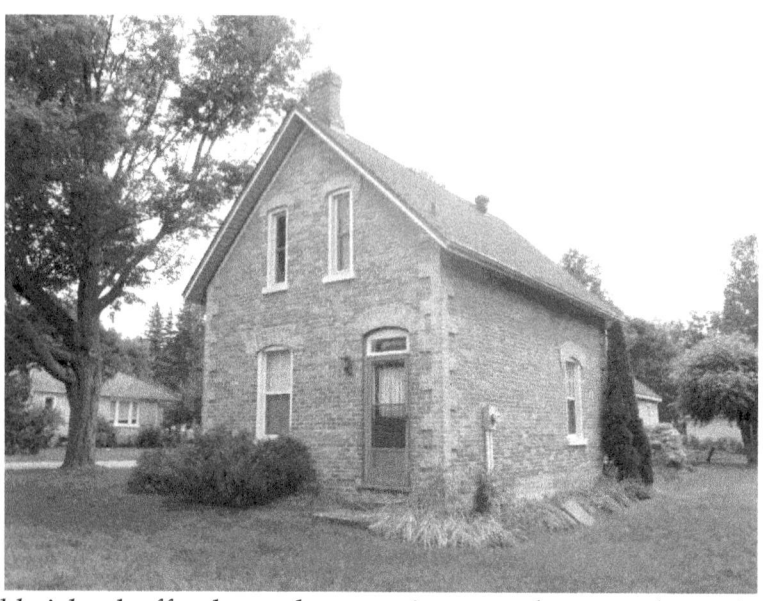

Red brick – buff coloured voussoirs over doors and windows, quoins on corners – Gothic Revival style

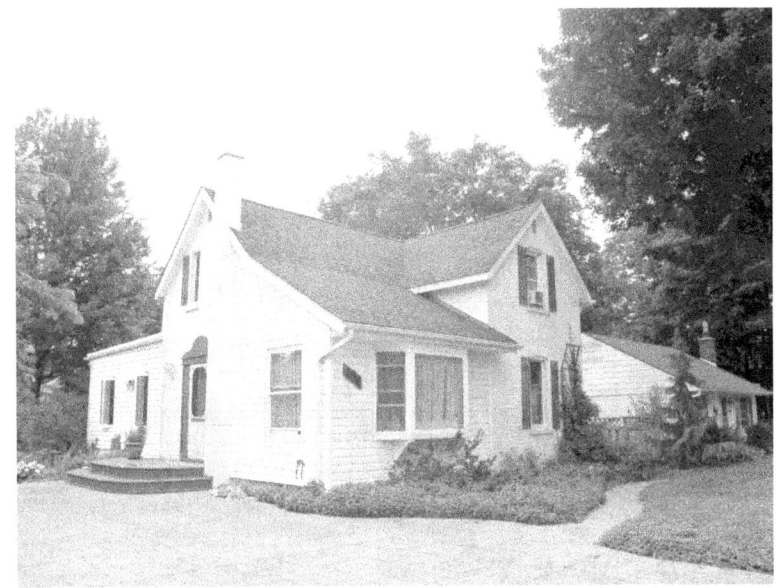

466 Elgin Street – Gothic Revival

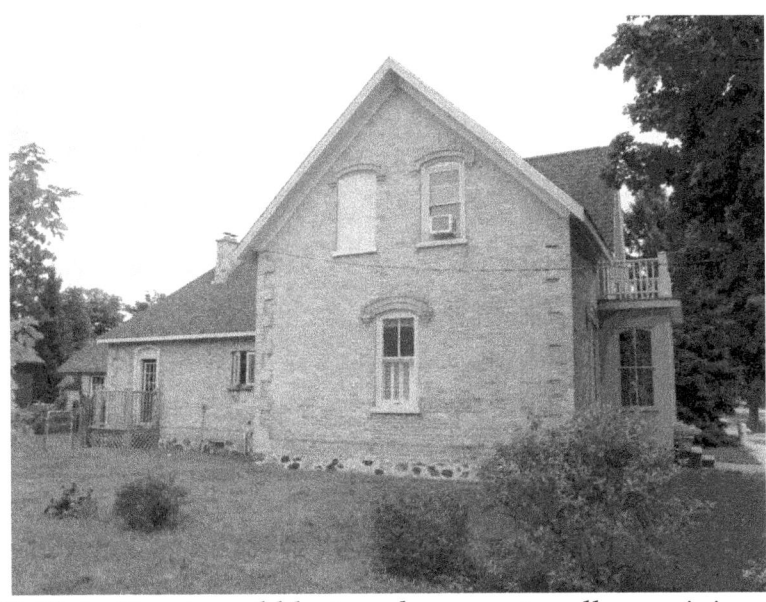

481 Elgin Street – cobblestone basement walls, quoining on corners, arched window voussoirs – yellow brick

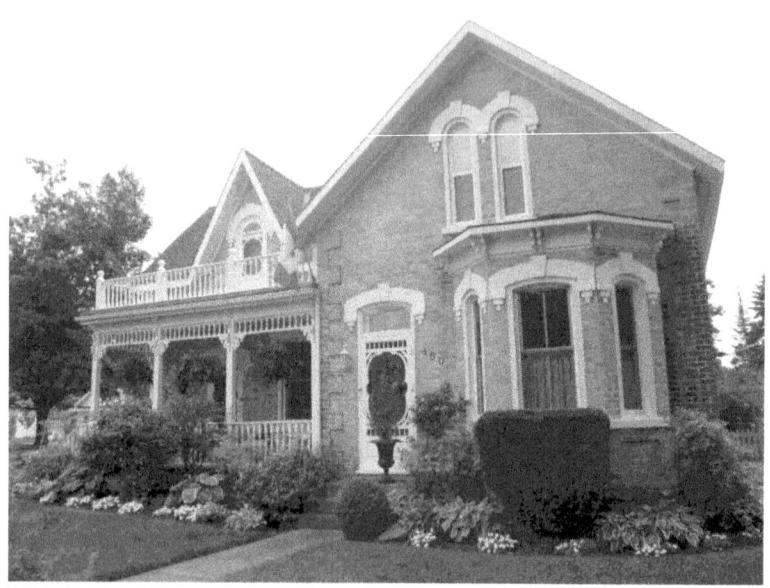

480 Market Street – yellow brick – Gothic Revival, arched voussoirs and keystones, bay window with cornice brackets

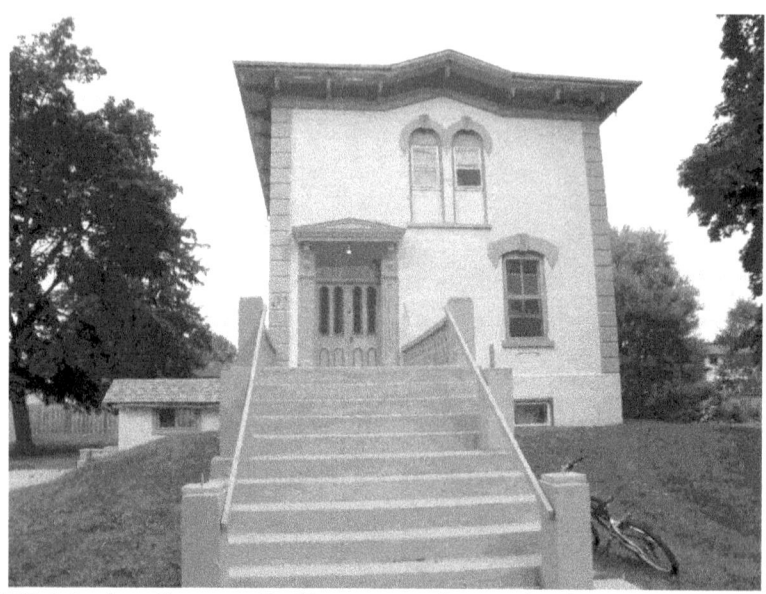

473 Market Street - Italianate style, arched voussoirs and keystones

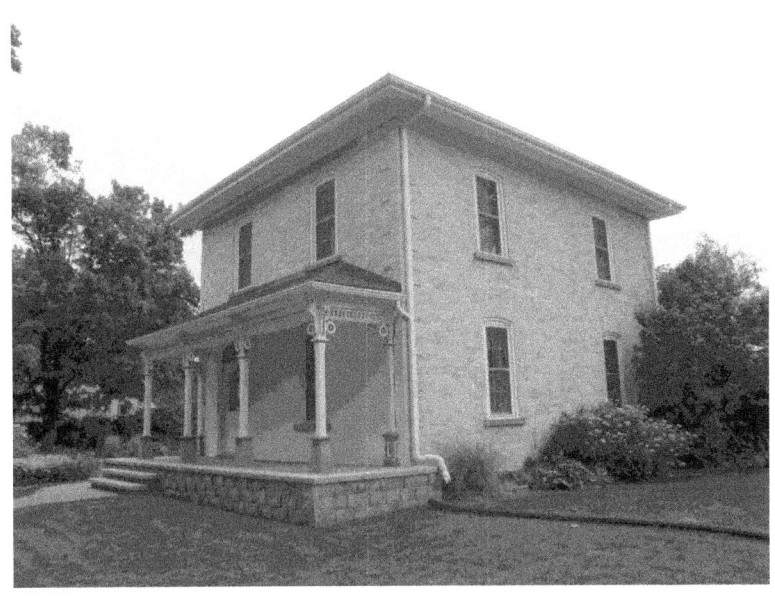

490 Market Street – yellow brick, Italianate style, corner quoins

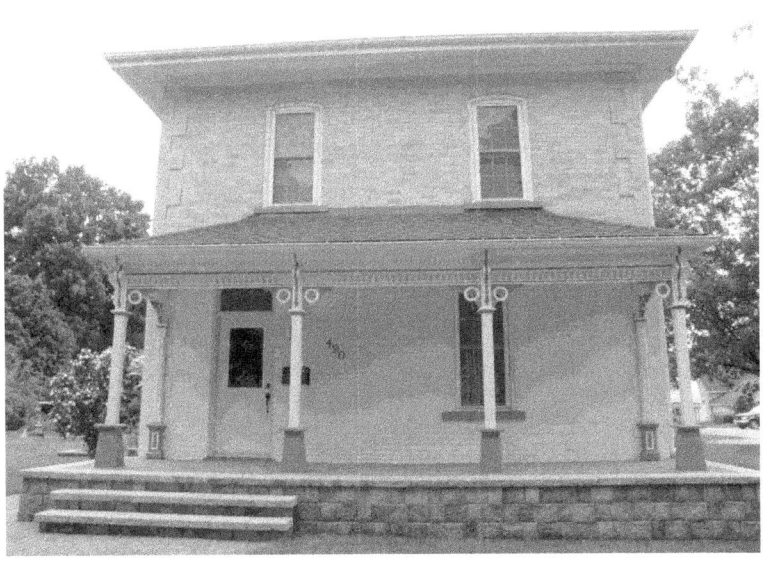

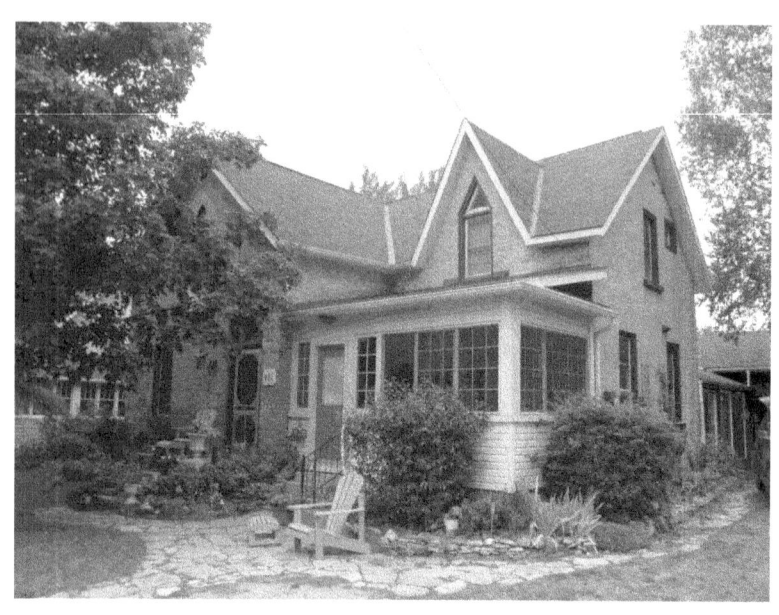

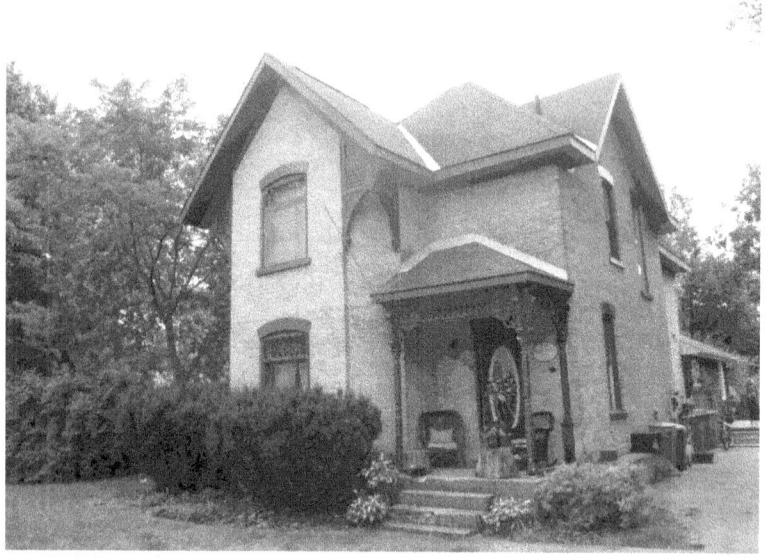

518 Market Street – Ernest Vaupel, Builder – 1890
Yellow brick - large fretwork pieces resembling brackets

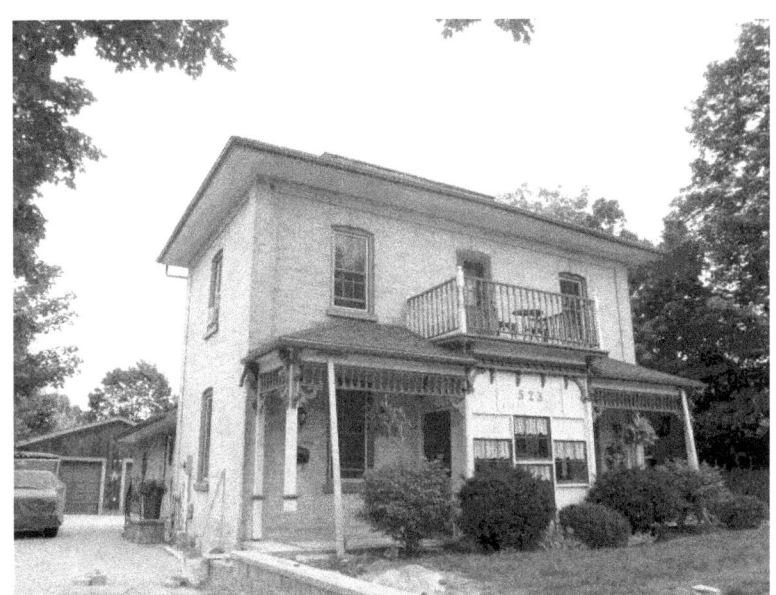

523 Market Street – yellow brick, Italianate style

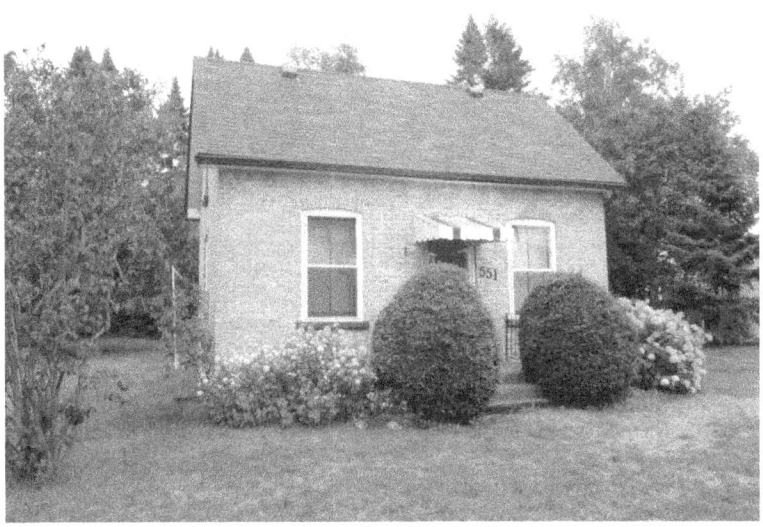

551 Market Street – Gothic Revival 1½ storey cottage

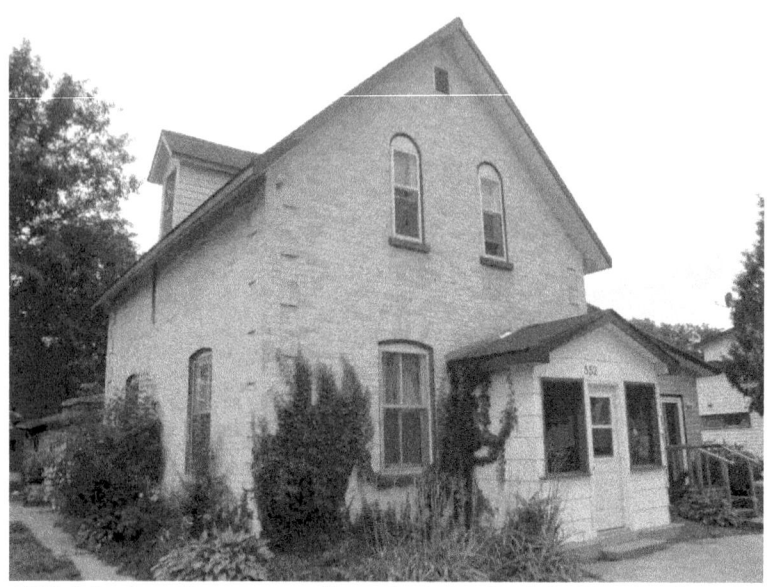

552 Market Street – yellow brick, Gothic Revival style

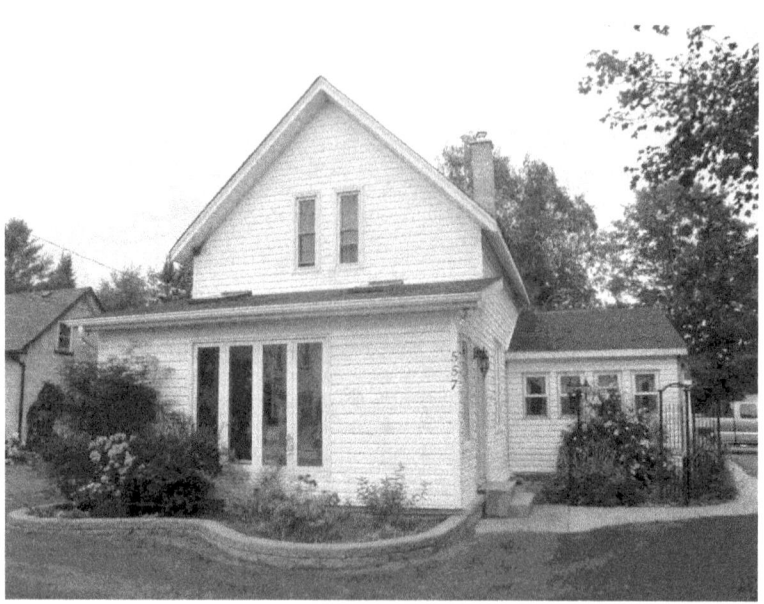

557 Market Street – Gothic Revival
– upgraded with white siding

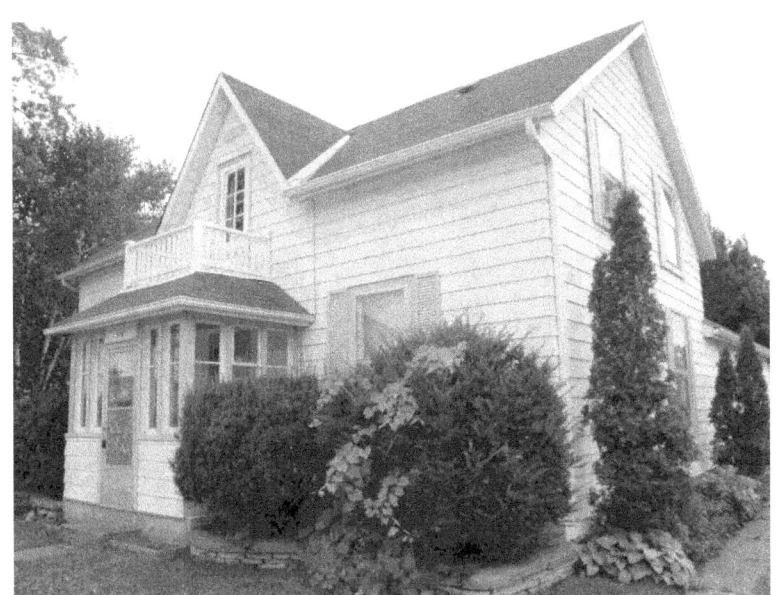

578 Market Street

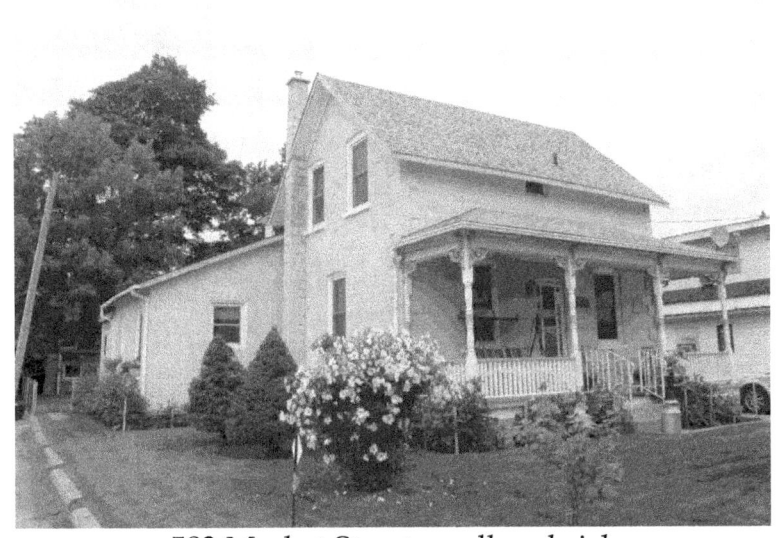

583 Market Street – yellow brick

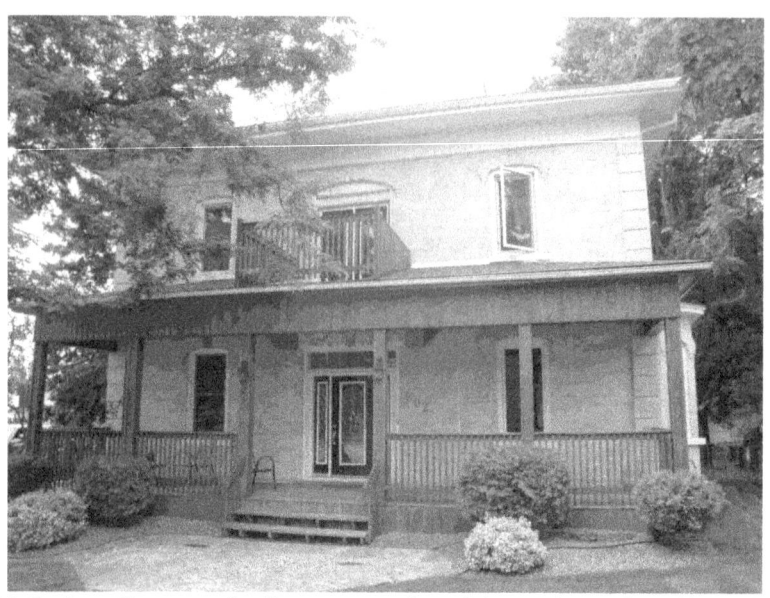
802 Market Street – Italianate style – hipped roof, yellow brick

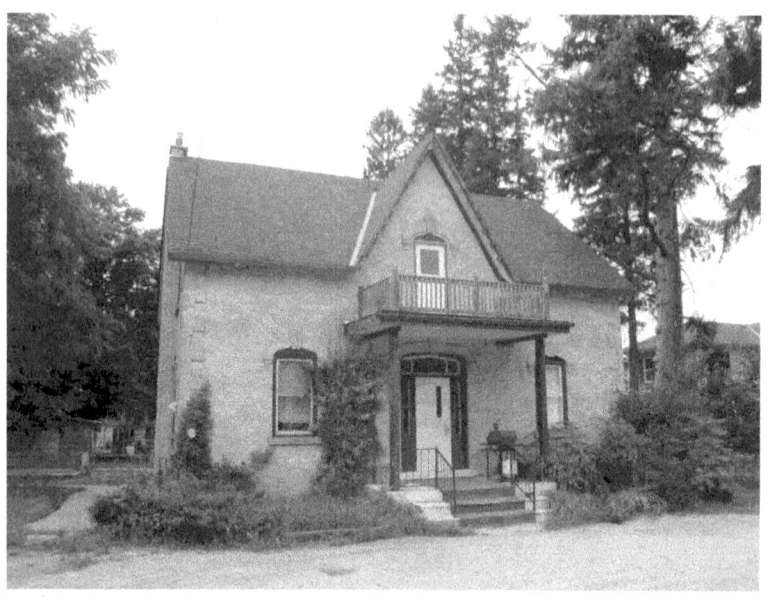
Gothic Revival cottage – arched voussoirs and keystones, corner quoins

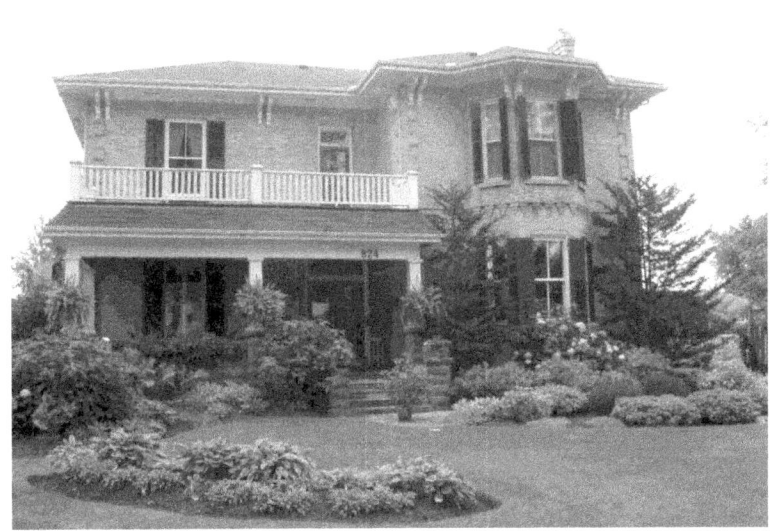

824 Goderich Street – Sprucehall Bed and Breakfast
Italianate style, paired cornice brackets

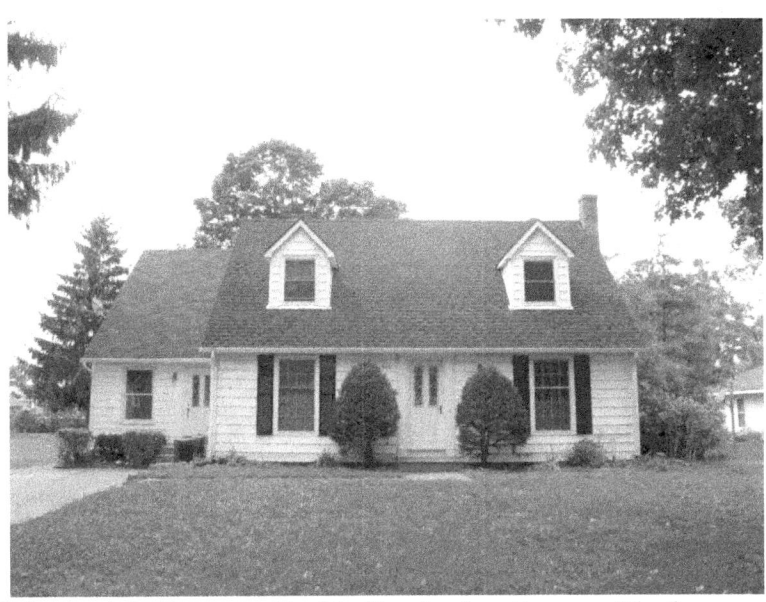

850 Goderich Street – Gothic Revival cottage with dormers in attic

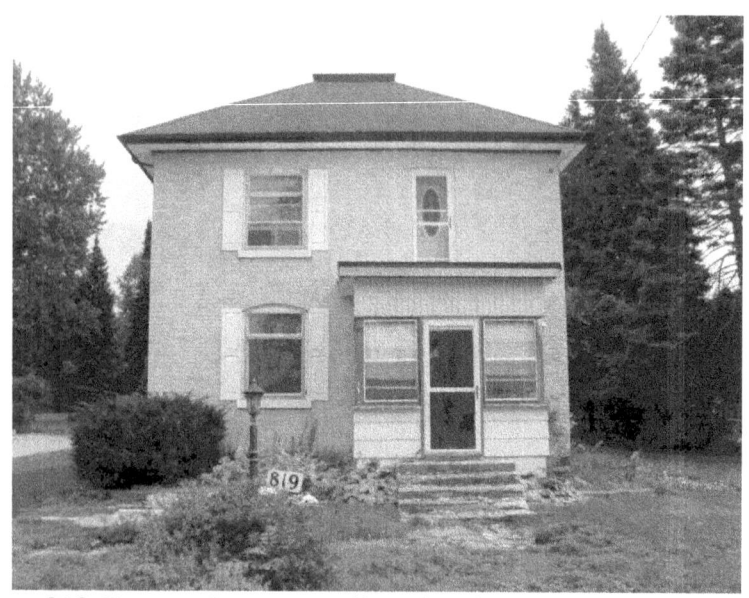
819 George Street – yellow brick, Italianate style

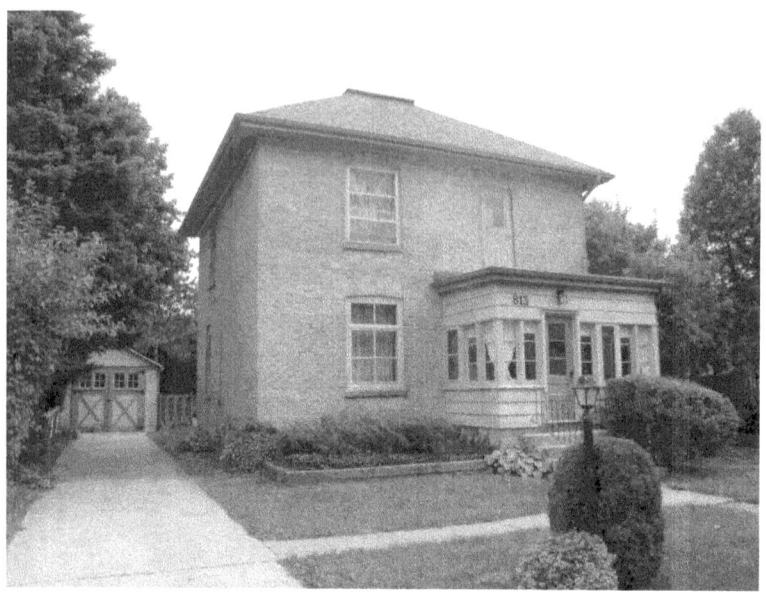
813 George Street – yellow brick

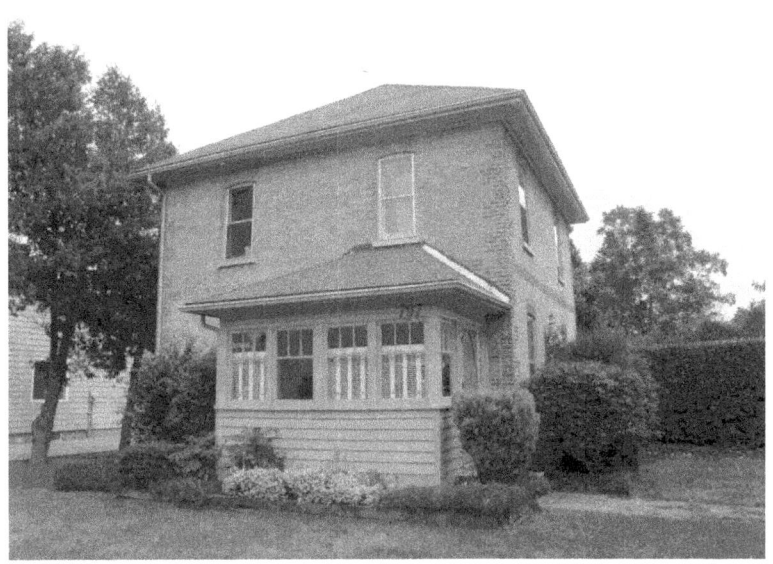

797 George Street – corner quoins, Italianate style

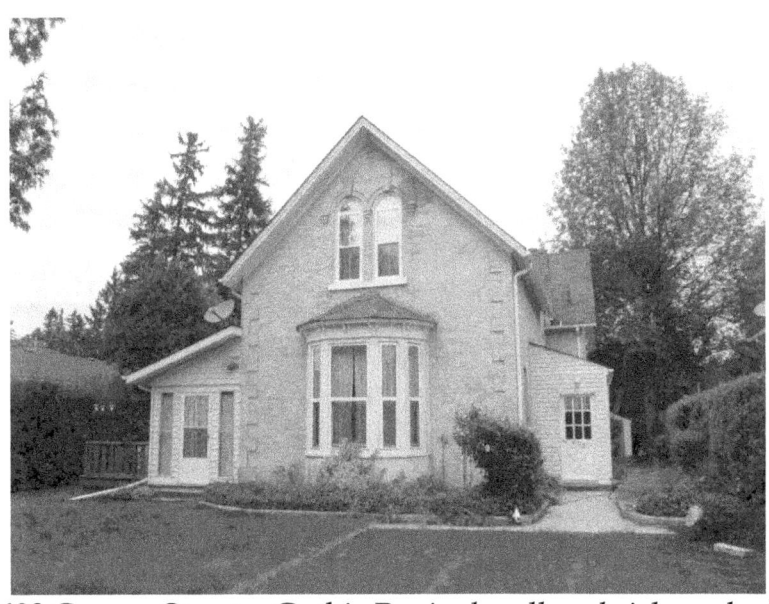

609 George Street – Gothic Revival, yellow brick, arched voussoirs and keystones, bay window with cornice brackets on roof

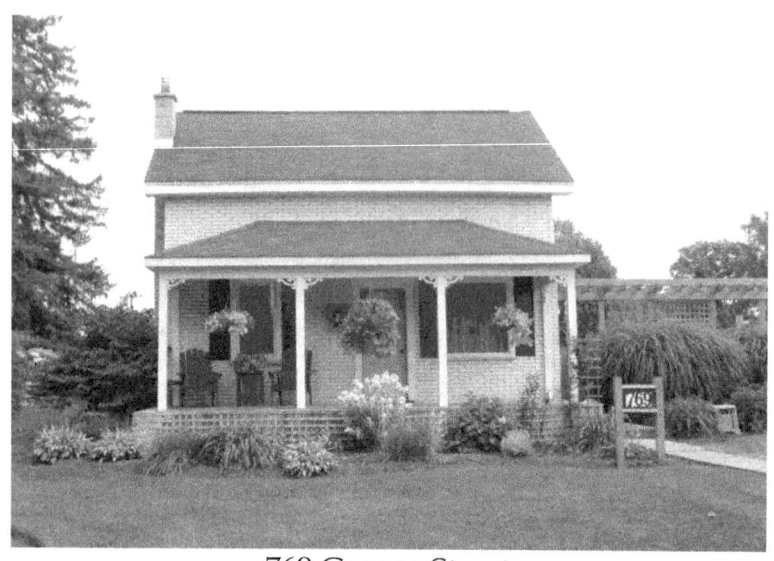

769 George Street

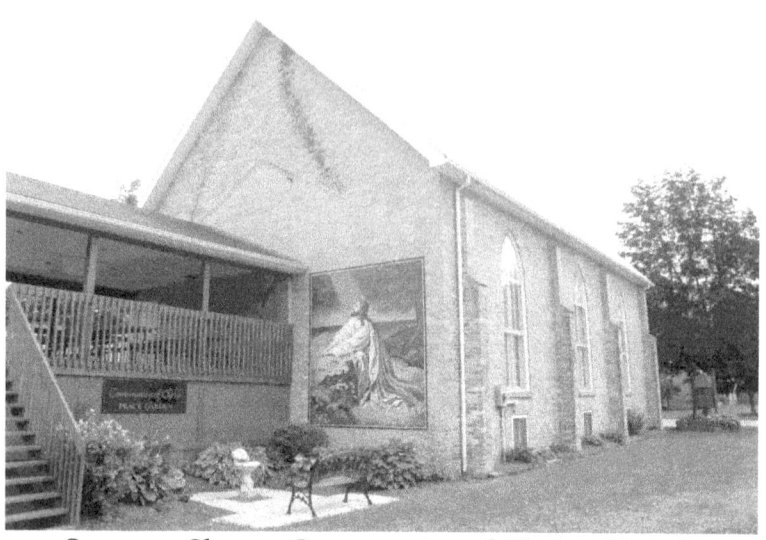

Saugeen Shores Community of Christ Church
641 Market Street at corner of Bricker – yellow brick, Gothic Revival

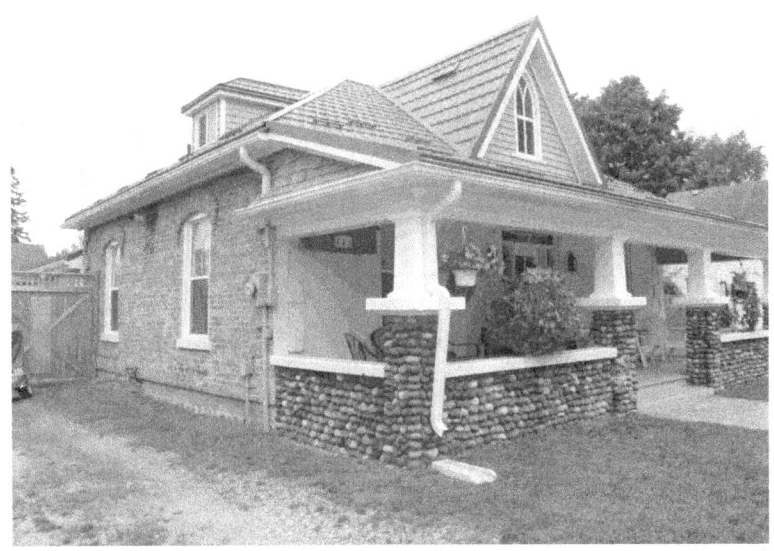

649 Market Street – yellow brick, Italianate cottage with dormer on side, and arched gable above verandah

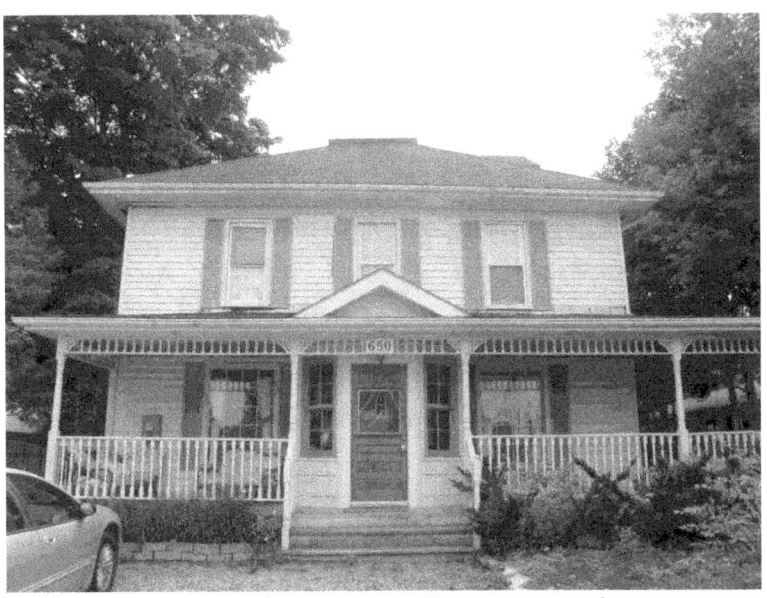

650 Market Street - Georgian style

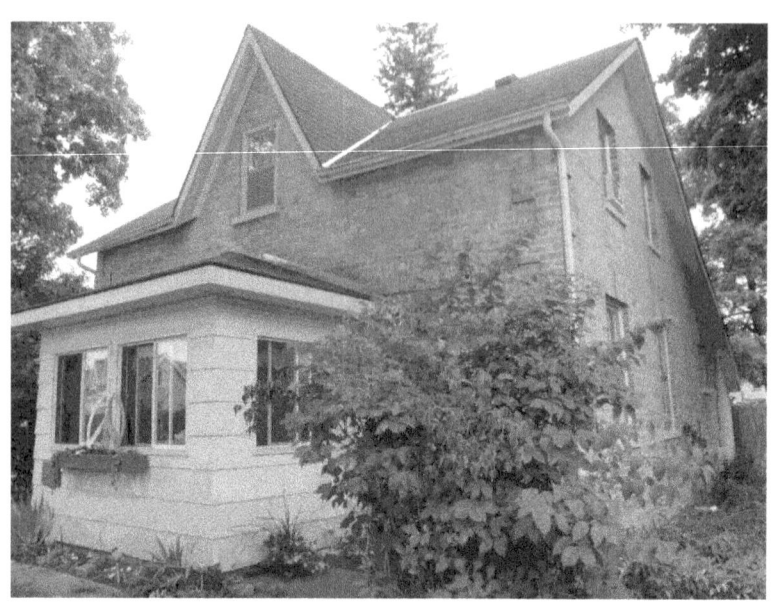

656 Market Street – Gothic Revival – 1½ storeys, corner quoins, yellow brick

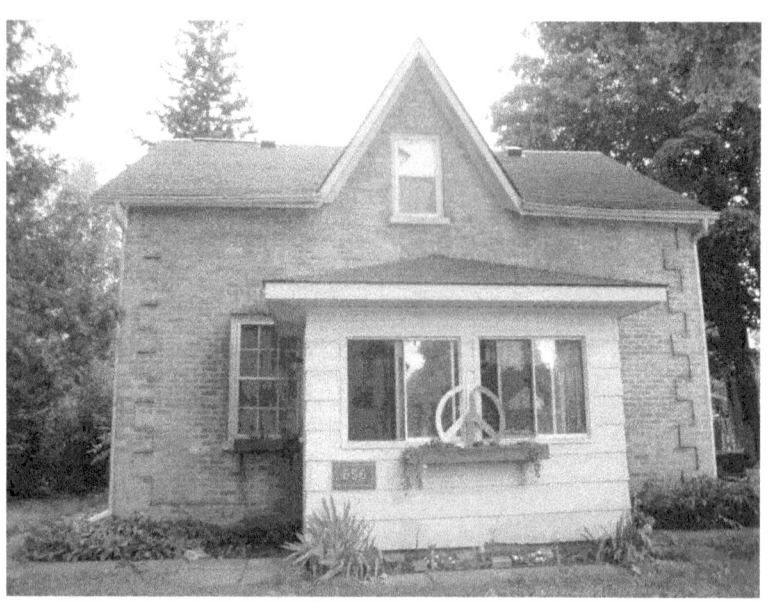

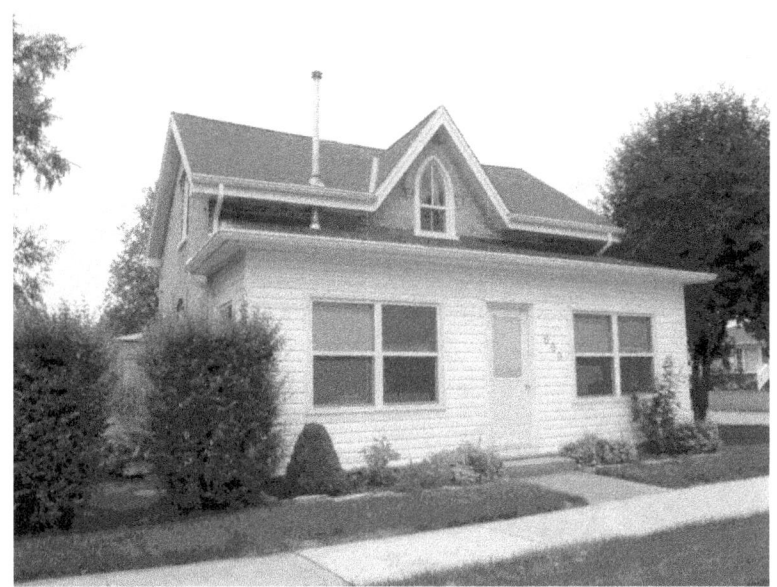

669 Market Street – Gothic cottage – lancet window in gable, original yellow brick

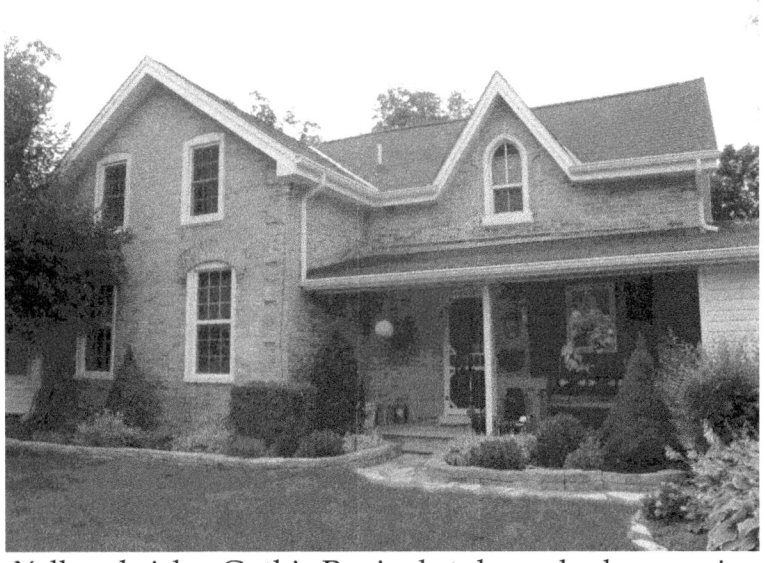

Yellow brick – Gothic Revival style, arched voussoirs

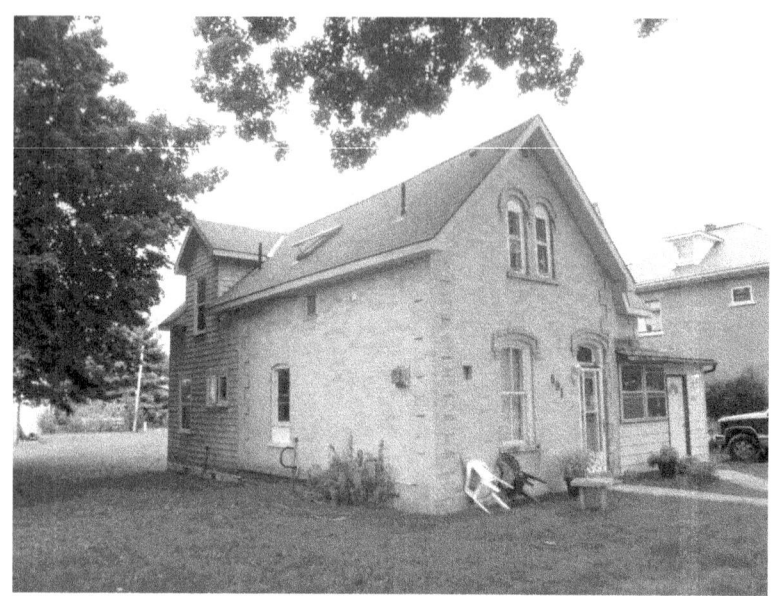

691 Market Street – yellow brick, Gothic Revival, 1½ storey, decorative voussoirs, corner quoins

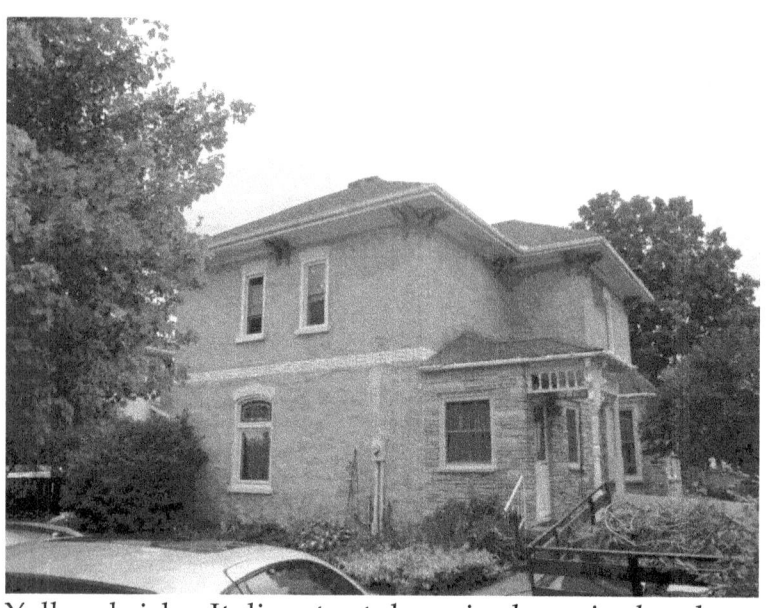

Yellow brick – Italianate style, paired cornice brackets, dichromatic banding, buff coloured voussoirs

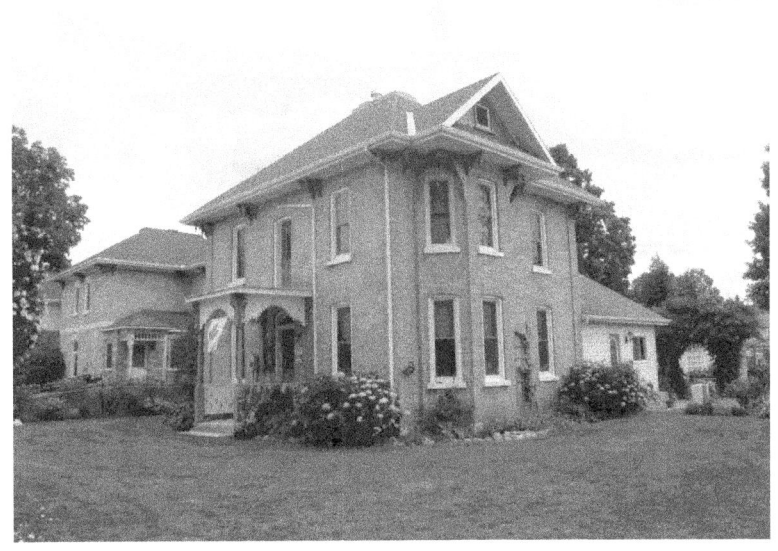

684 Market Street – John C. Kennedy, Grain Dealer – circa 1877 – yellow brick, Italianate style, paired cornice brackets

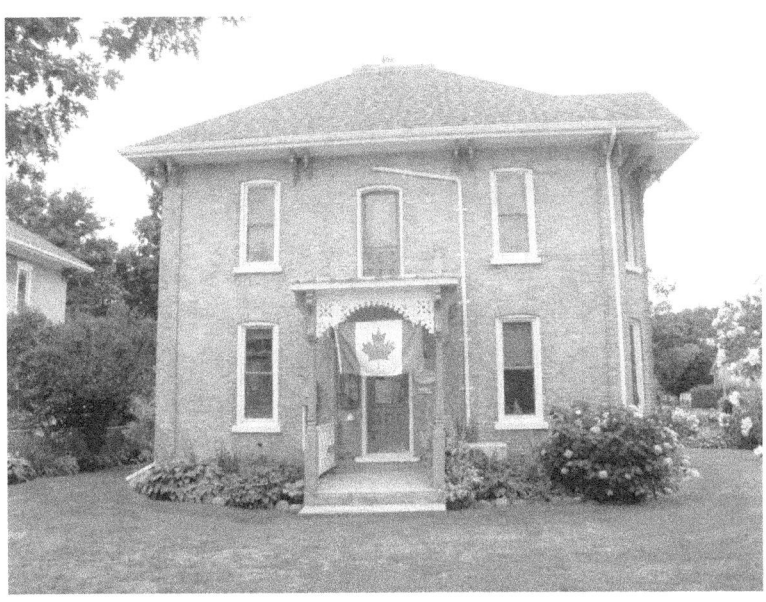

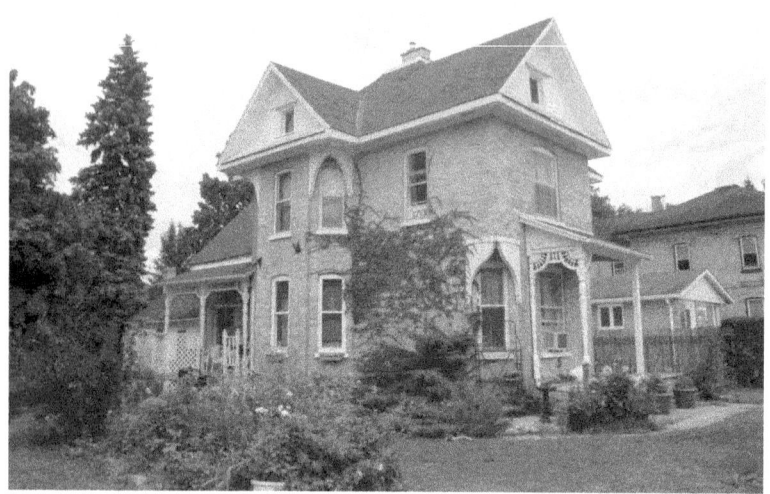

Yellow brick – Gothic Revival/Italianate - two-and-a-half storey tower-like bay with projecting eaves and large fretwork pieces resembling brackets – matching fretwork piece over lower window to left of porch and below porch roof

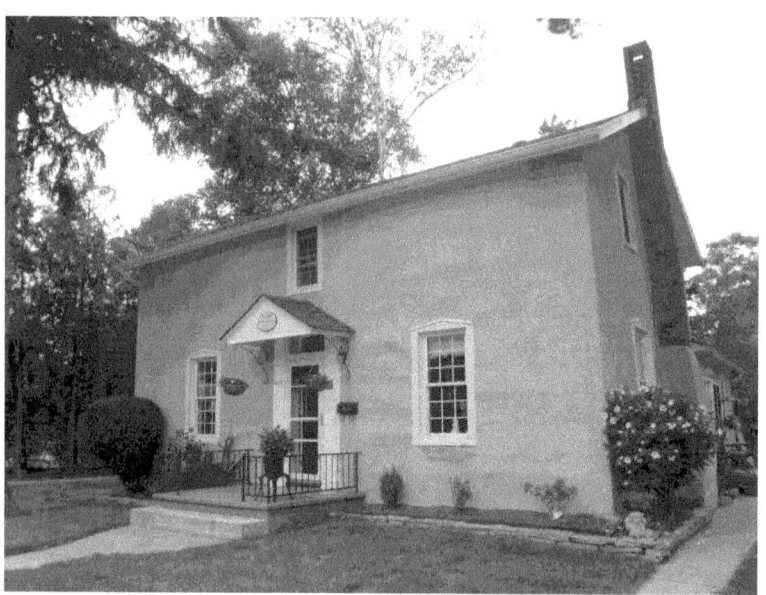

660 Hilker Street – Samuel Roether, Gaoler – c. 1870 – stucco

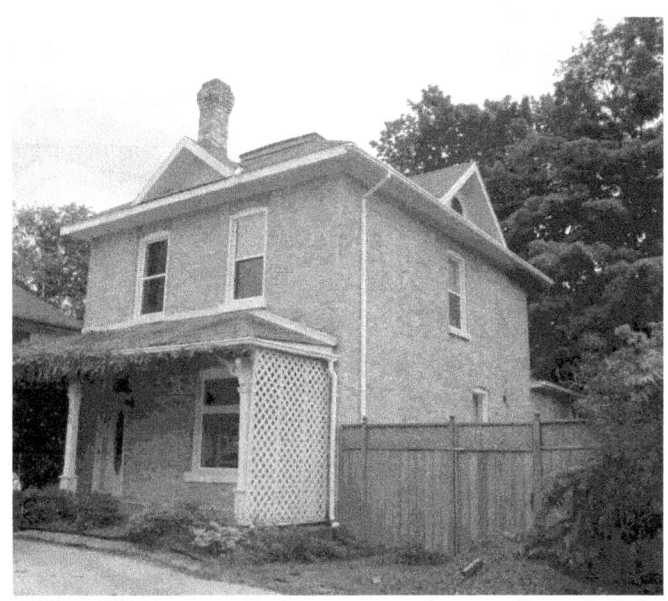

700 Mill Street - Italianate style – yellow brick

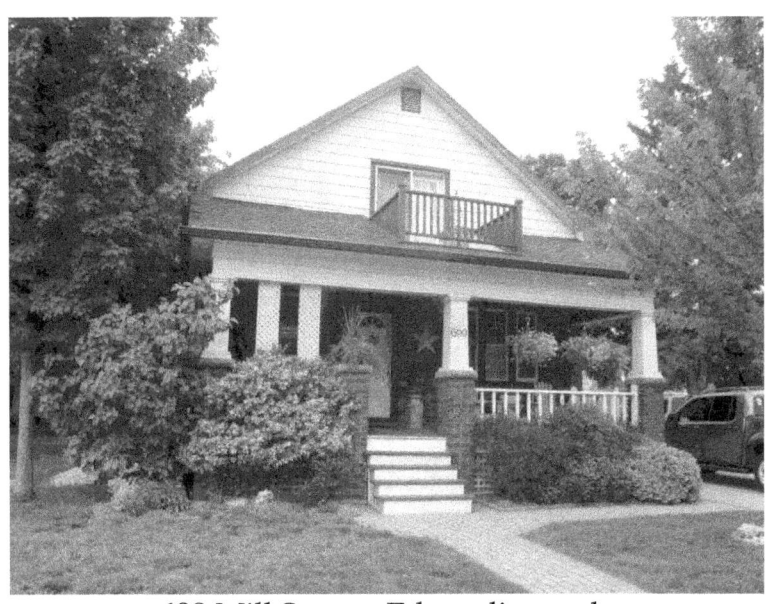

699 Mill Street - Edwardian style

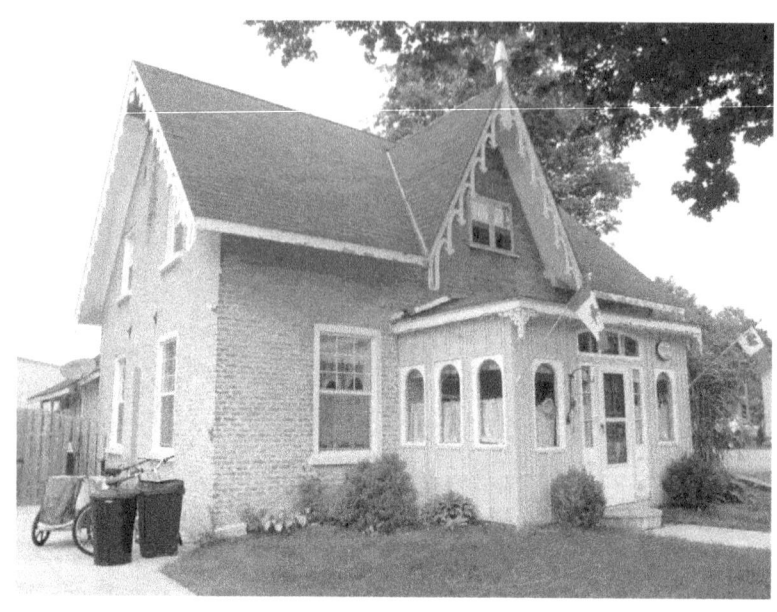

709 Mill Street – Gothic Revival – Vergeboard trim on gables – yellow brick

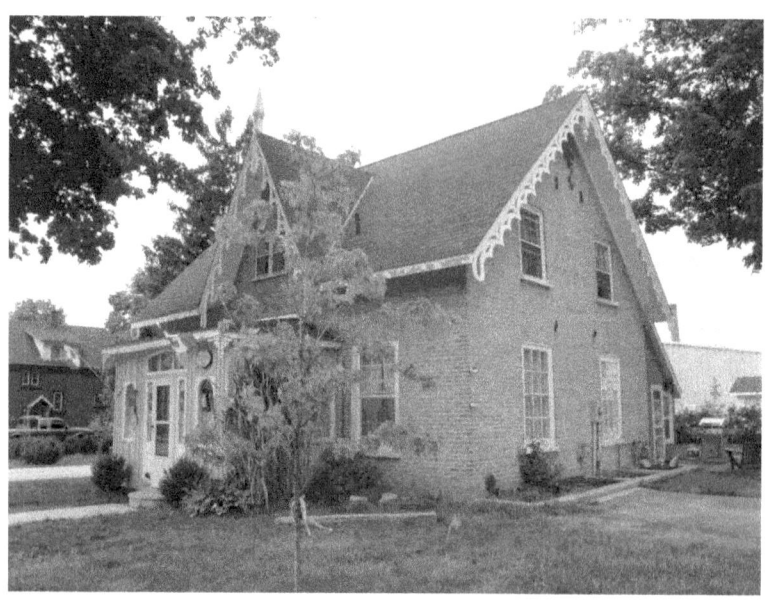

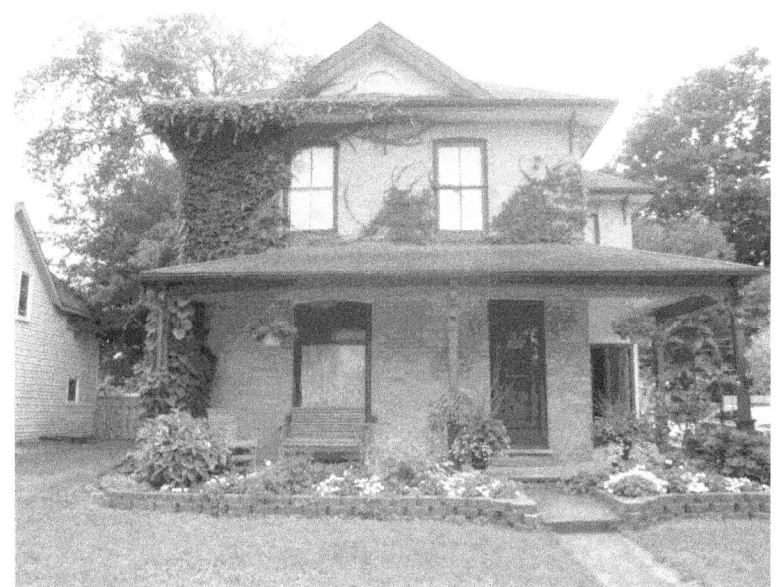

706 Mill Street – Italianate style – yellow brick

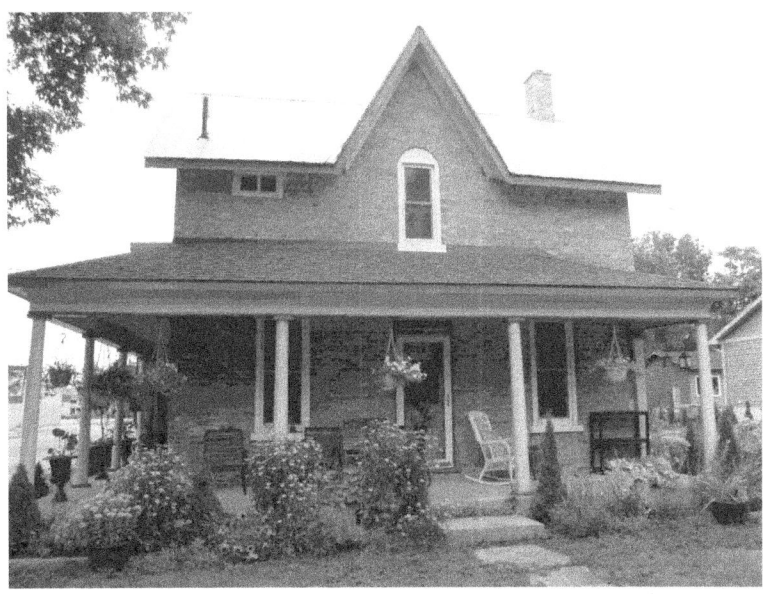

Gothic Revival – 1½ storey, yellow brick

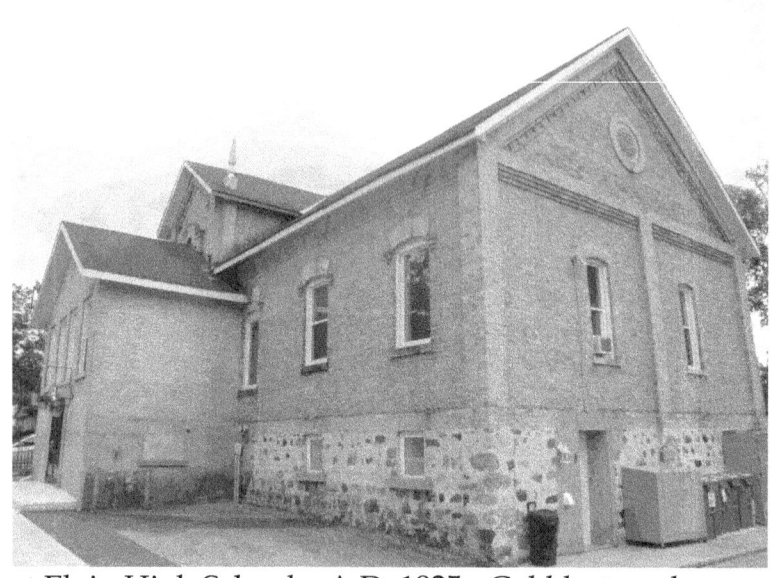

Port Elgin High School – A.D. 1925 - Cobblestone basement
Yellow brick, dentil moulding on gable end, arched voussoirs
742 Mill Street

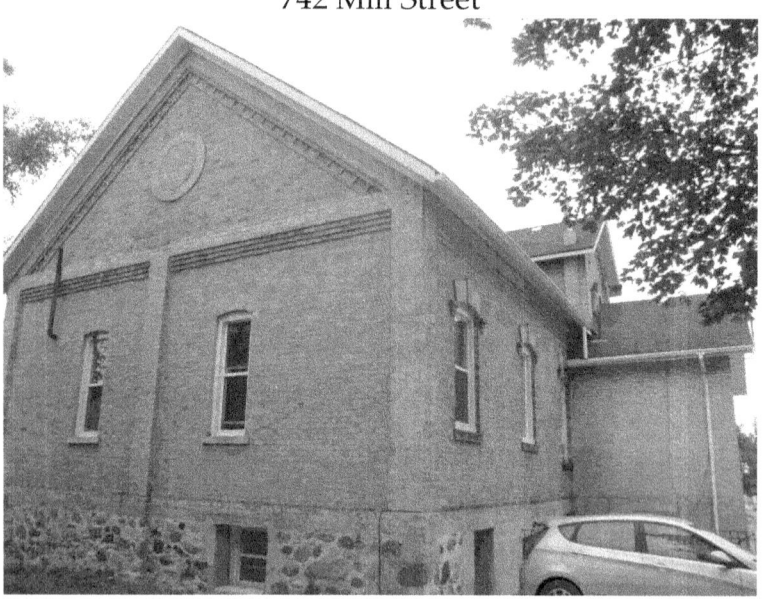

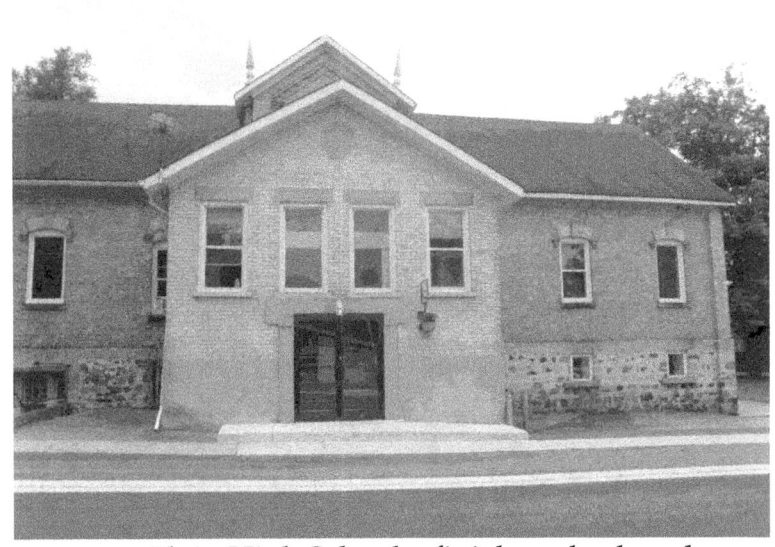

Port Elgin High School – finials on back arch

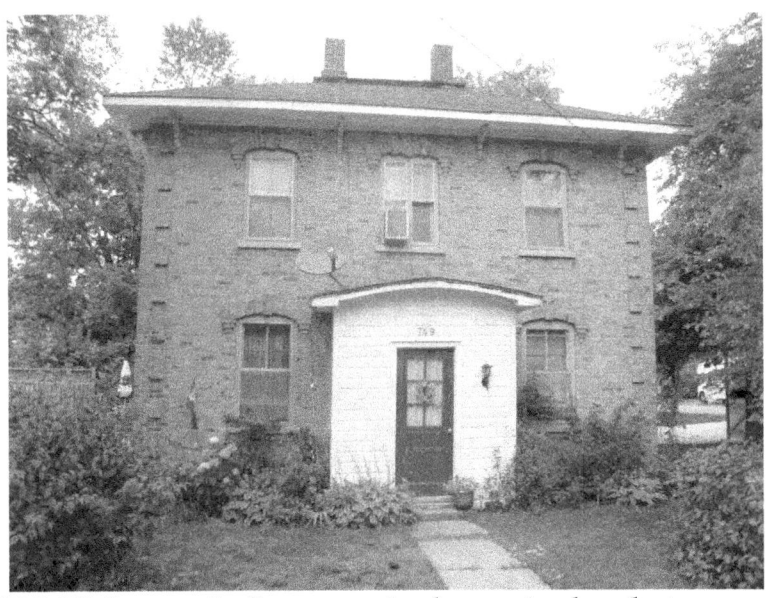

749 Mill Street – Italianate – single cornice brackets, corner quoins, decorative voussoirs

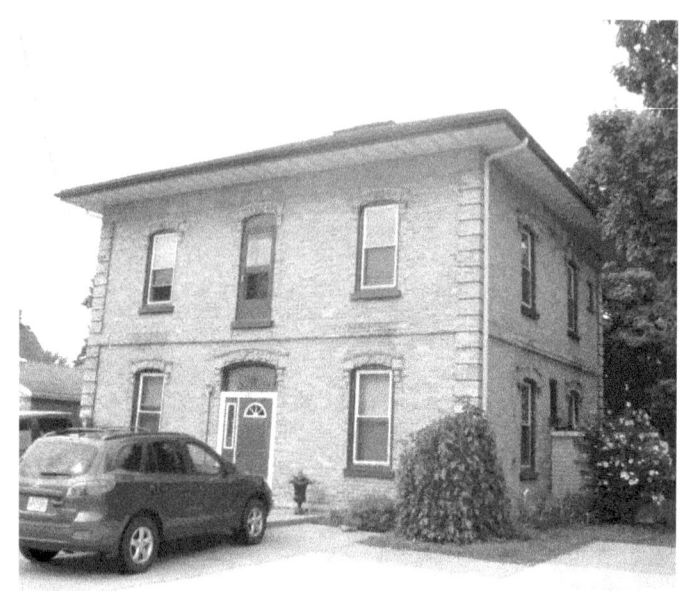

695 Mill Street – Italianate, corner quoins, decorative voussoirs

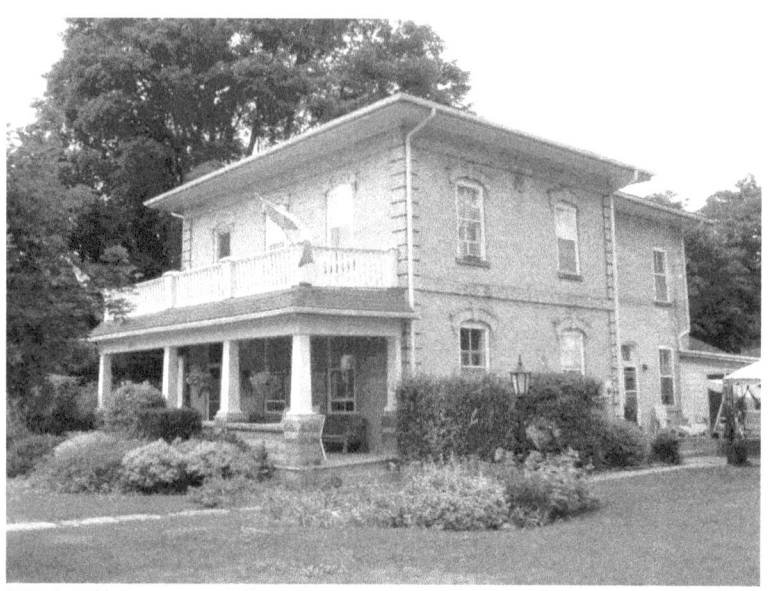

657 Mill Street – The George House Bed and Breakfast - Italianate style

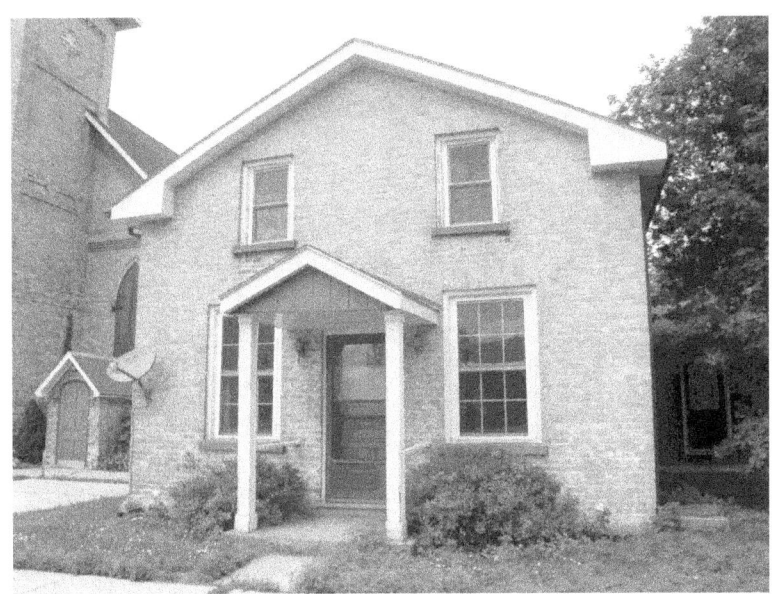

Gothic Revival, yellow brick, cornice return on gable

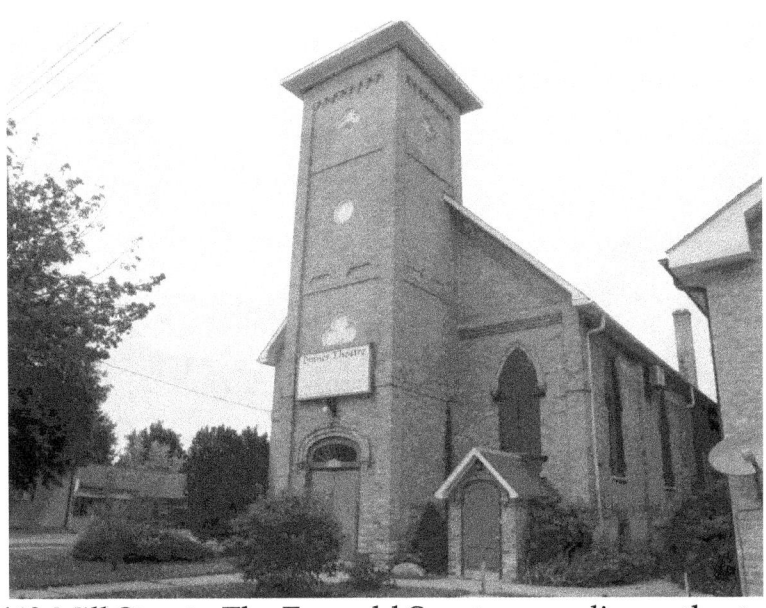

643 Mill Street - The Emerald Sanctuary – dinner theatre – yellow brick

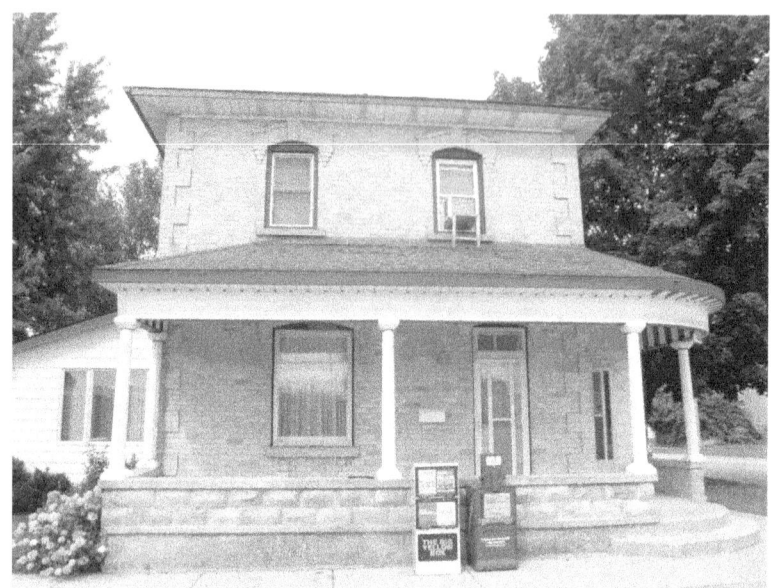

Italianate – yellow brick, decorative voussoirs and keystones, corner quoining

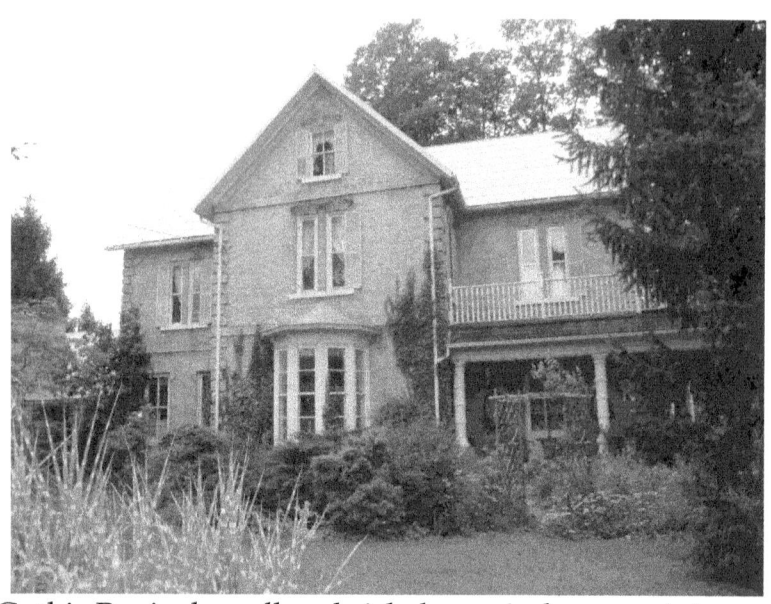

Gothic Revival – yellow brick, bay window, quoining on corners, decorative voussoirs and keystones

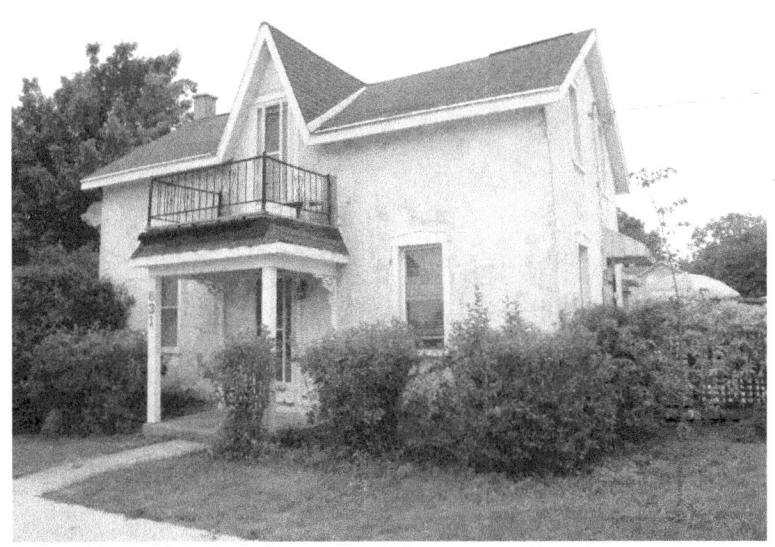

632 Catherine Street – 1½ storey Gothic cottage – plaster exterior

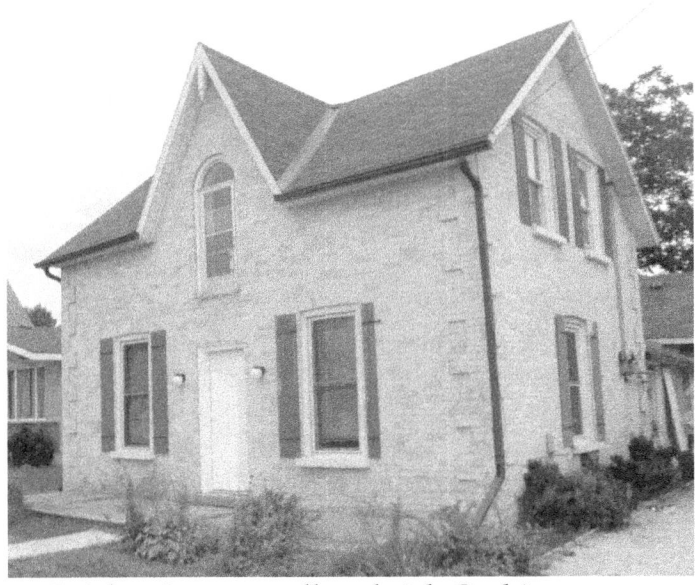

Bricker Street – yellow brick Gothic cottage

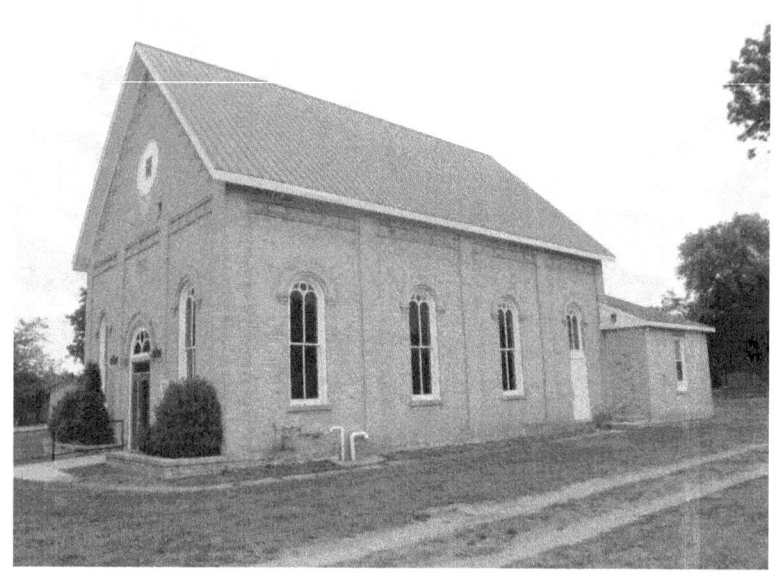

Regular Baptist Church A.D. 1878

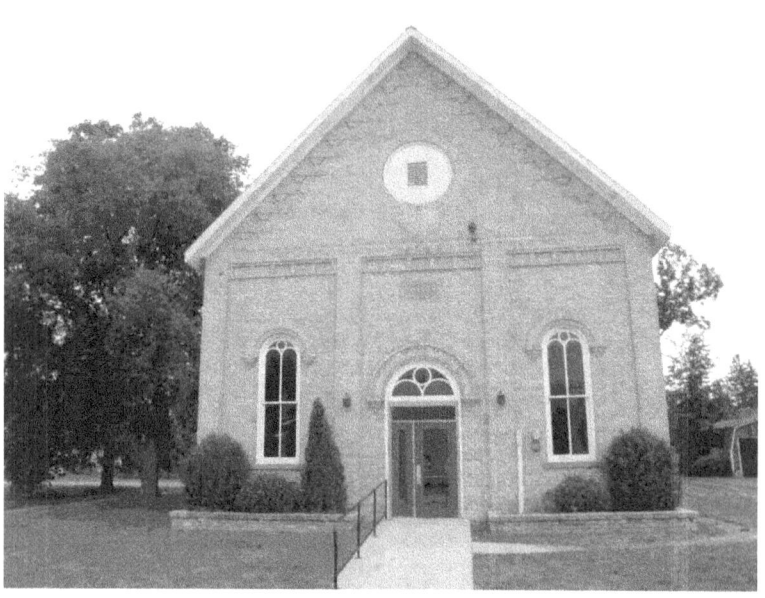

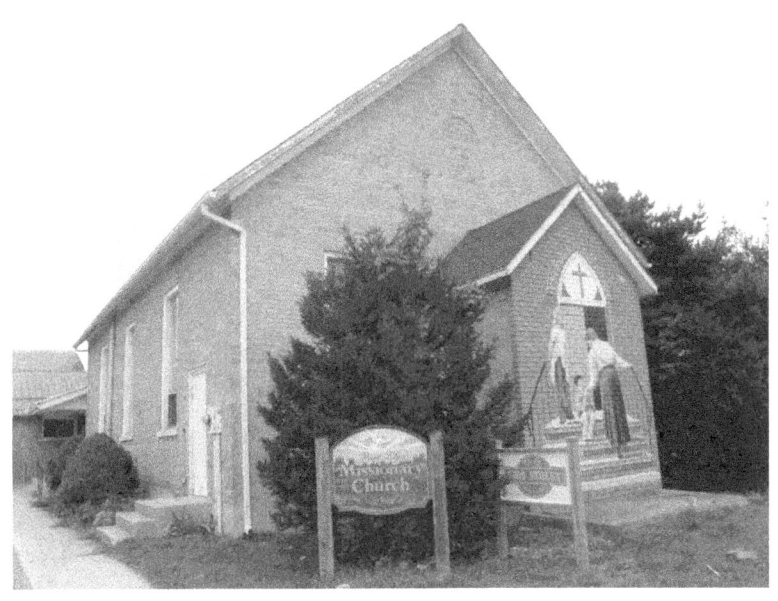

Port Elgin Missionary Church (United Mennonite Church A.D. 1875) – 659 Gustavus Street

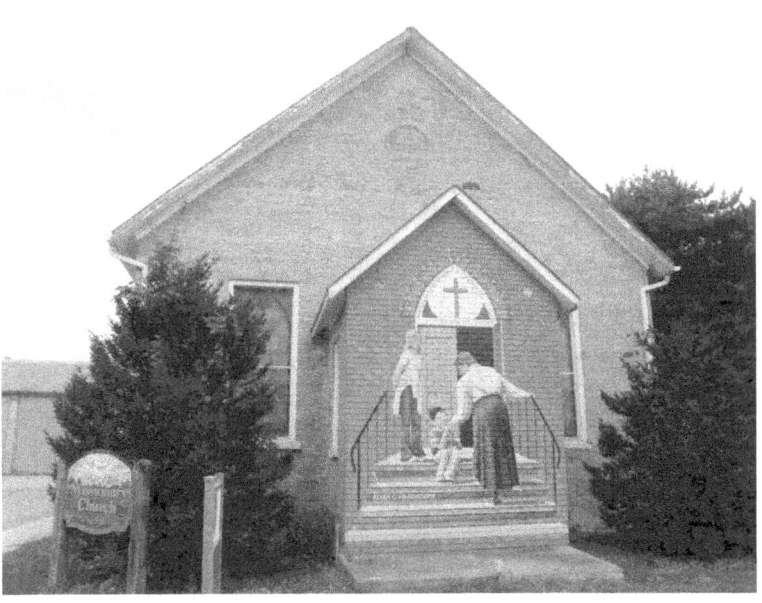

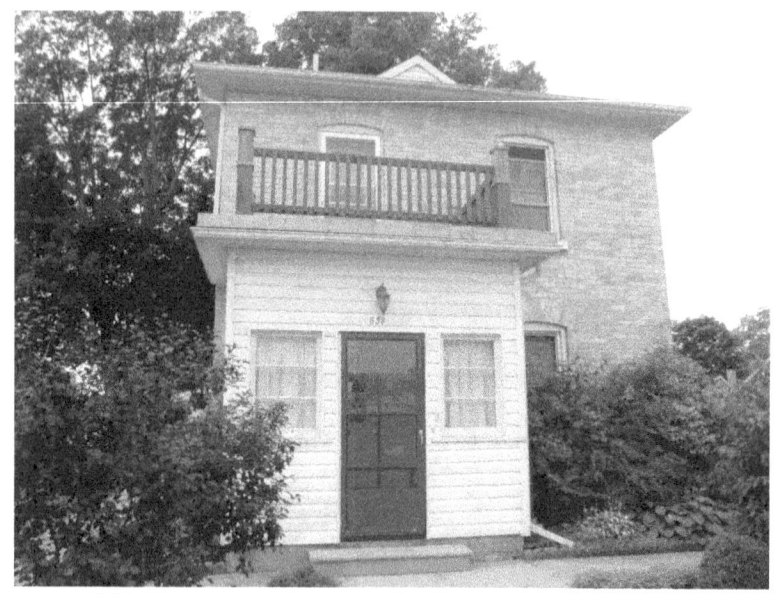

658 Gustavus Street – Italianate style - plain

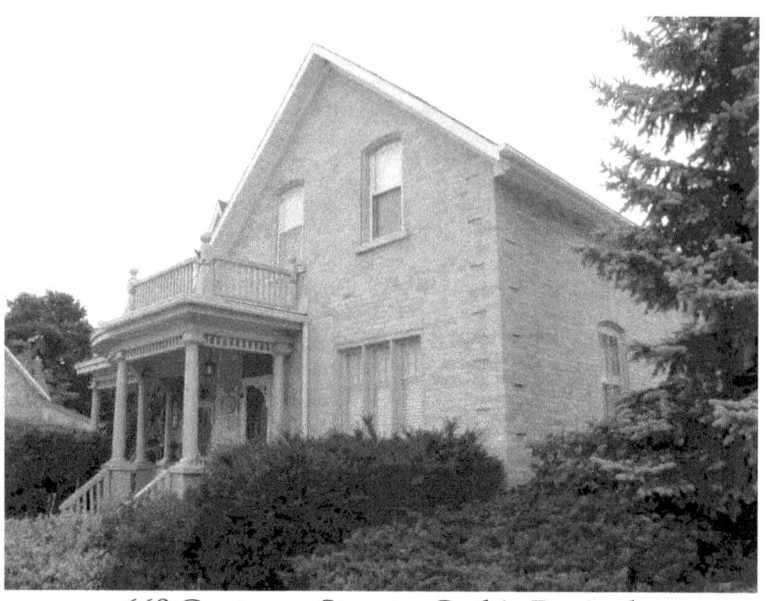

668 Gustavus Street – Gothic Revival

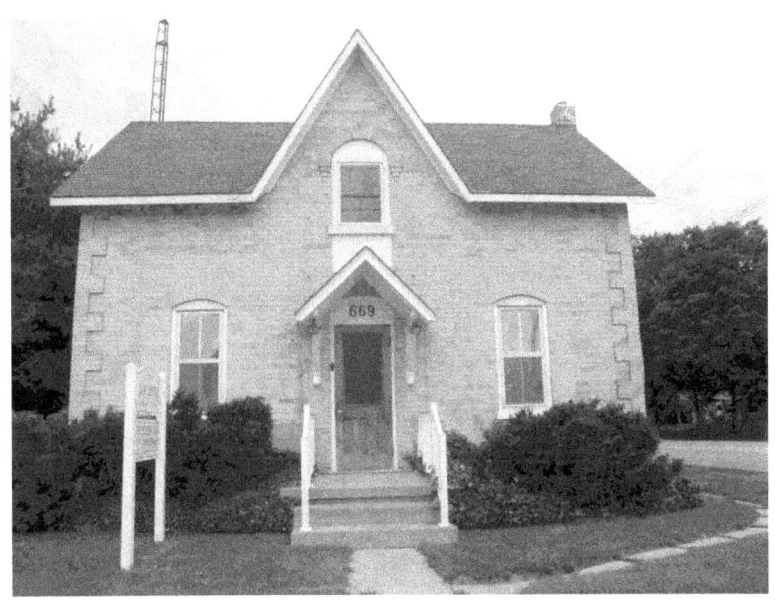

669 Gustavus Street – Gothic Revival Cottage
– arched voussoir over attic window, corner quoins

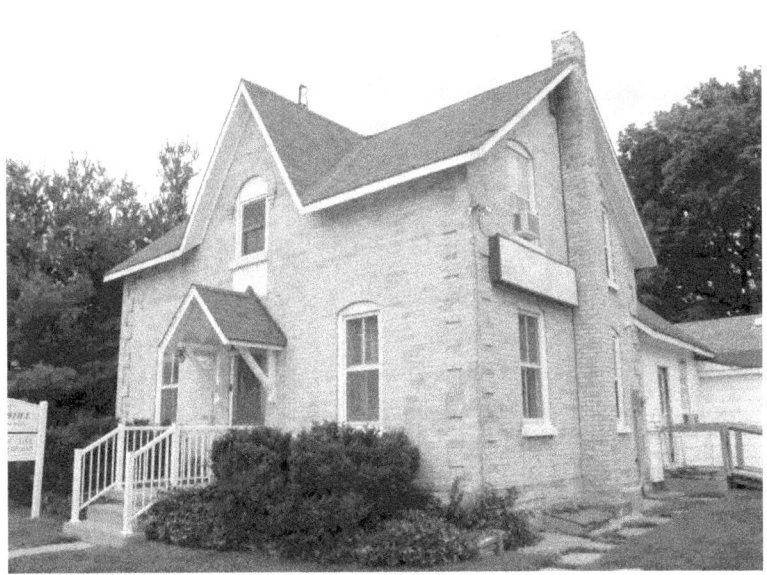

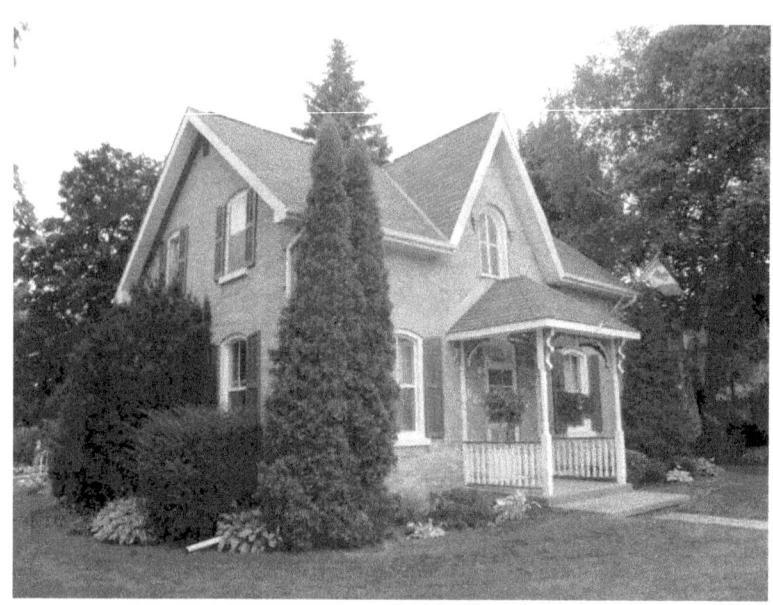

687 Gustavus Street – Gothic Revival – yellow brick

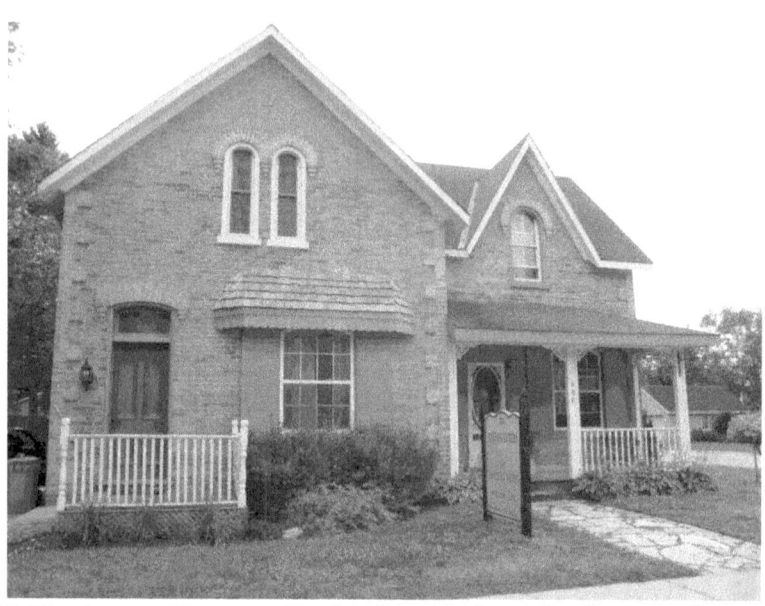

686 Gustavus Street – Gothic Revival, arched vousoirs over upper windows, corner quoining – red brick

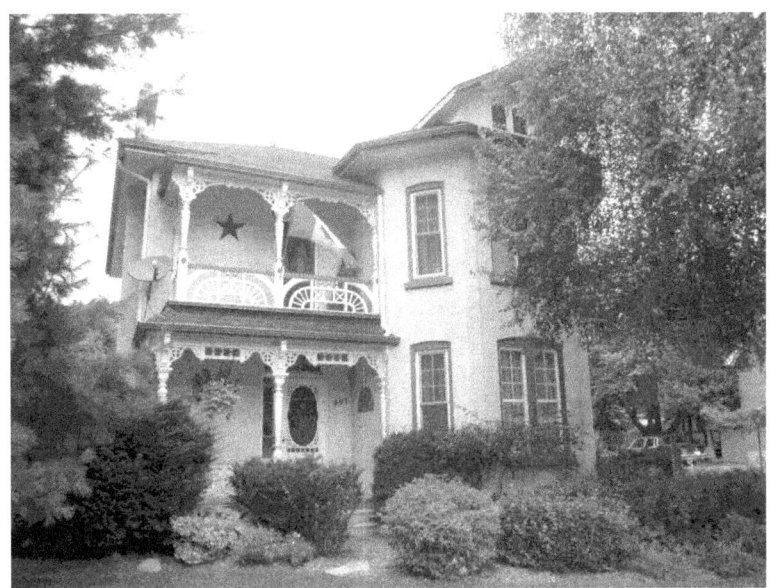

697 Gustavus Street – Italianate style – elaborate decorative fretwork on the balcony and porch

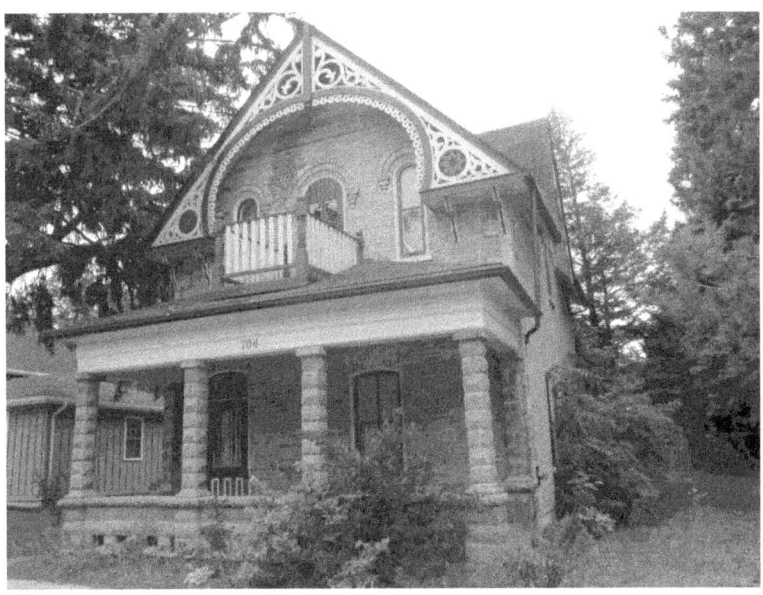

704 Gustavus Street – Gothic Revival – elaborate vergeboards, arched voussoirs – yellow brick

Hepworth

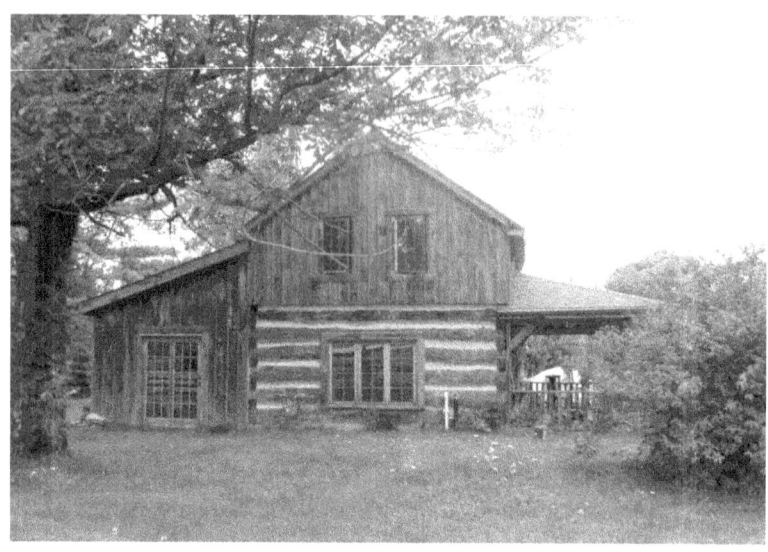

Log cabin

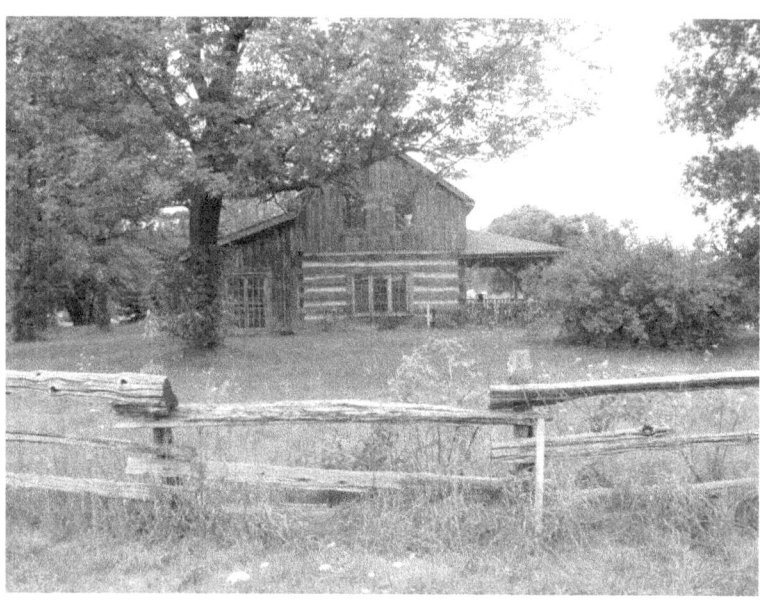

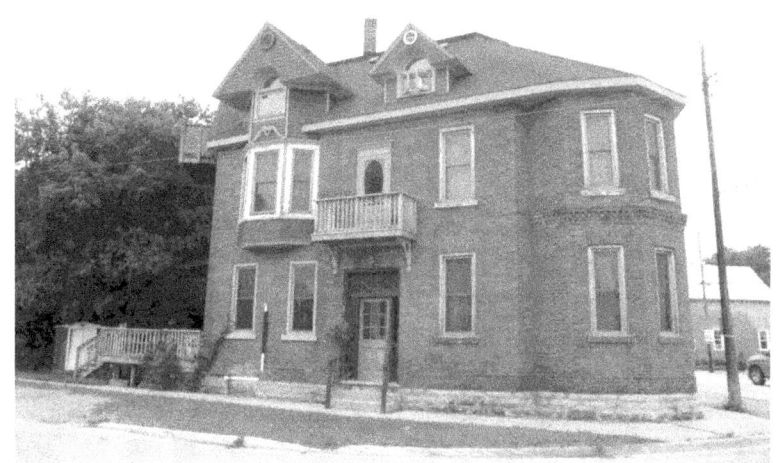

Red brick – Italianate – gabled dormers in attic, bay window on second storey

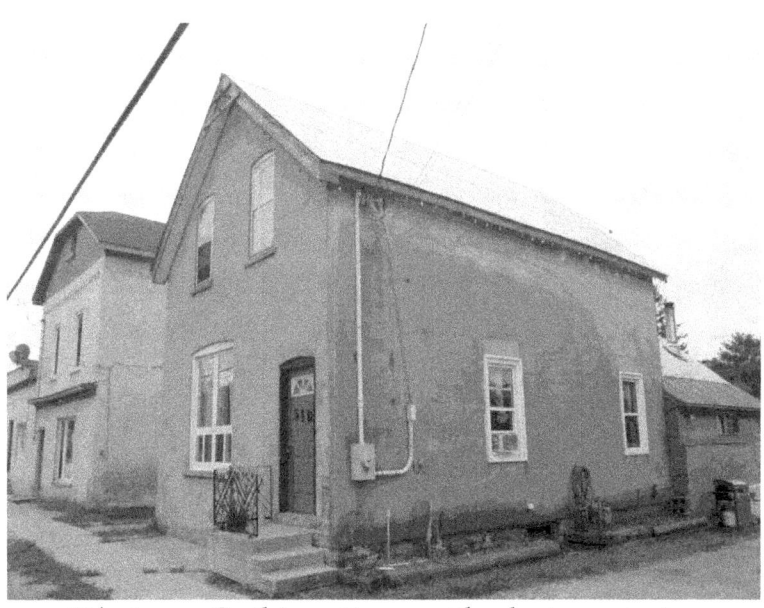

1½ storey Gothic cottage with plaster exterior

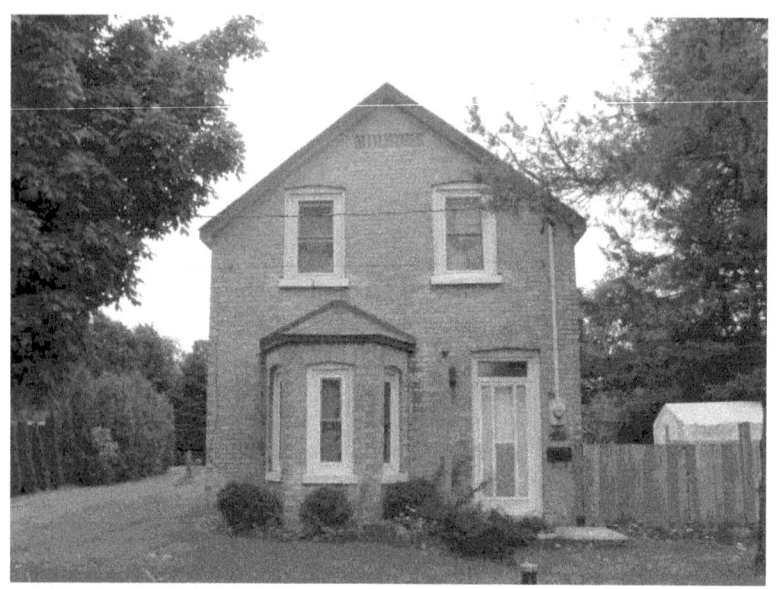

1½ storey yellow brick – Gothic Revival, bay window

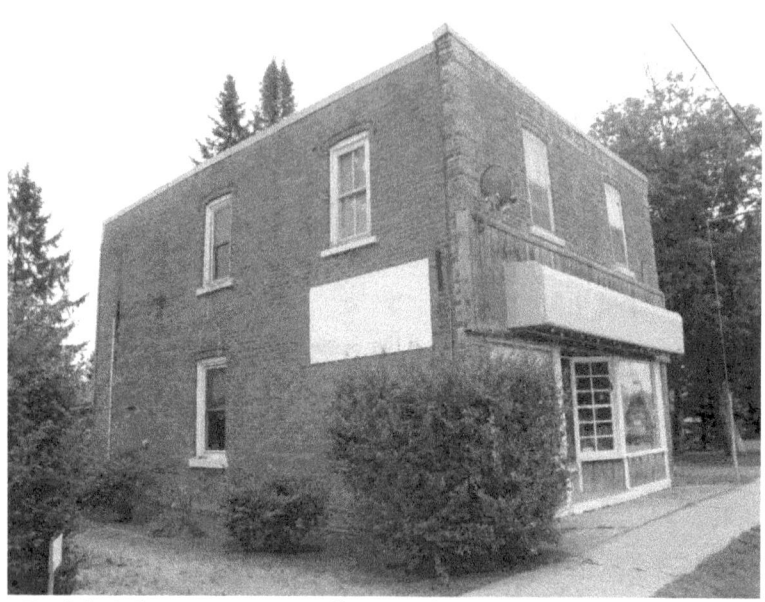

Red brick two-storey, flat roof building, dichromatic brickwork

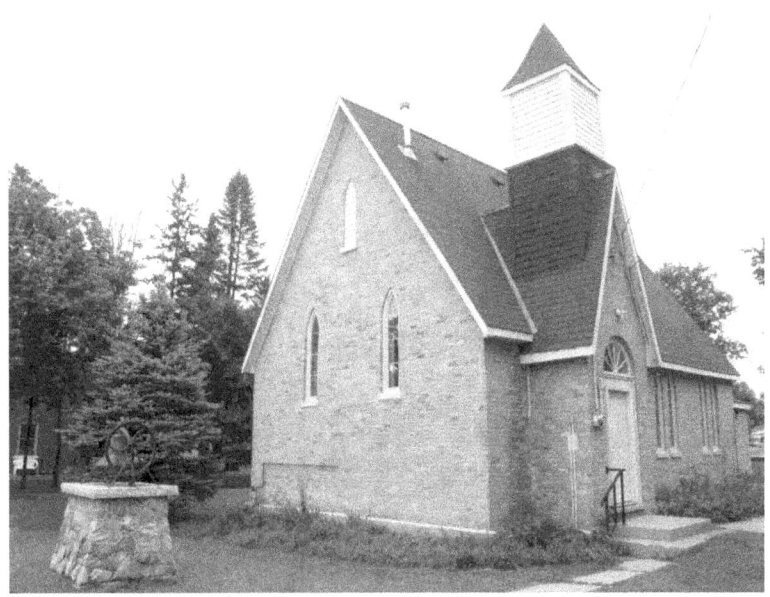

Anglican Church of the Redeemer – built 1886. From 1965 to 1997 is was the public library. In January 1998 it became the Community Centre for the village of Hepworth.

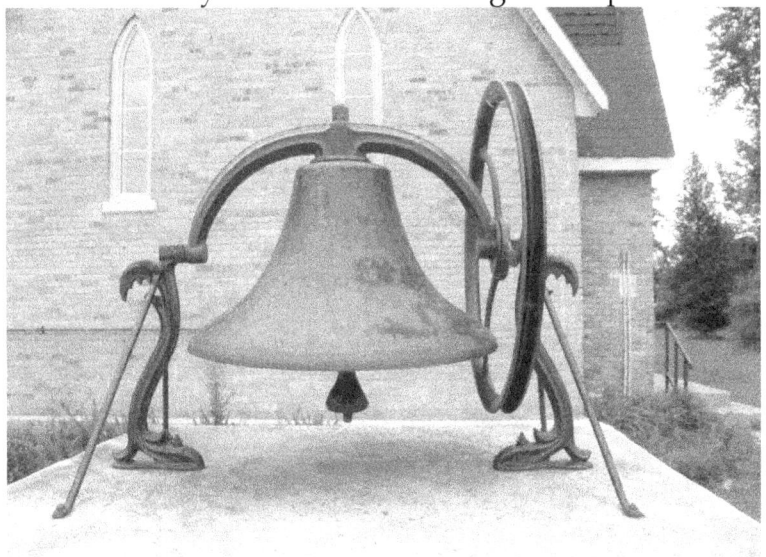

This bell was dedicated to the men and women who built the Anglican Church of the Redeemer in 1886 to 1965.

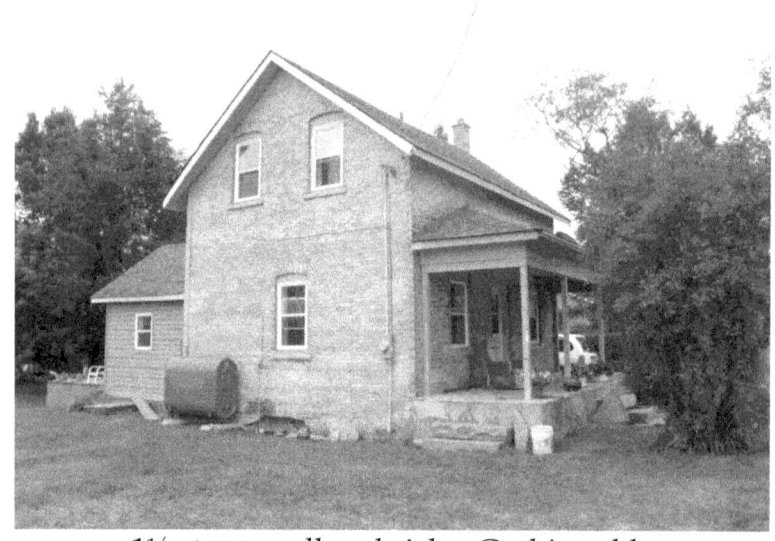

1½ storey yellow brick – Gothic gable

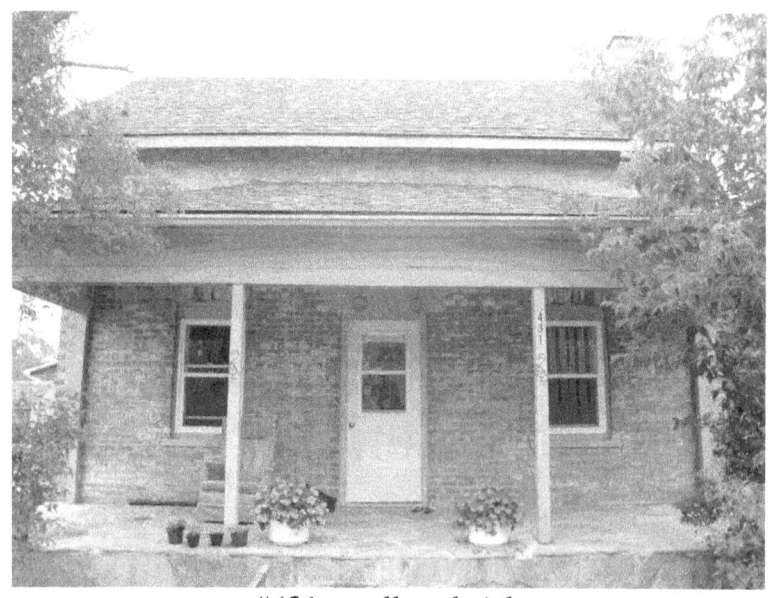

#431 – yellow brick

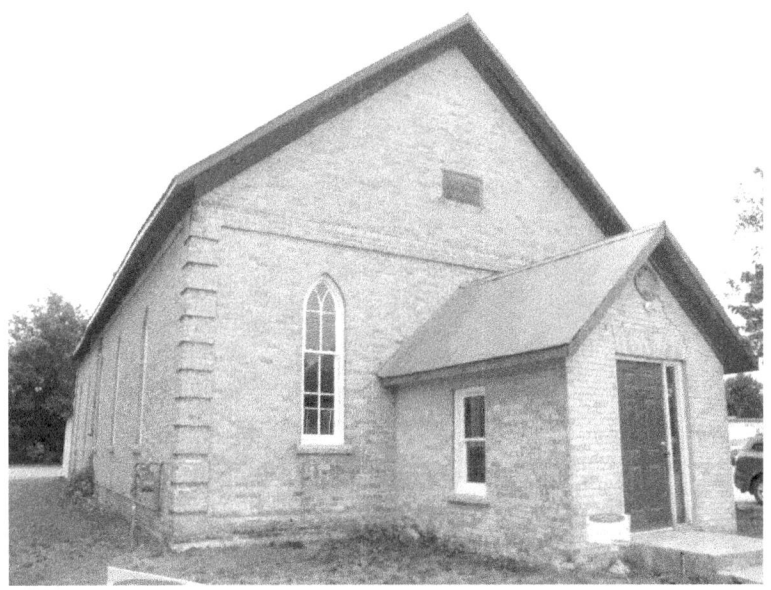

Hepworth Hall

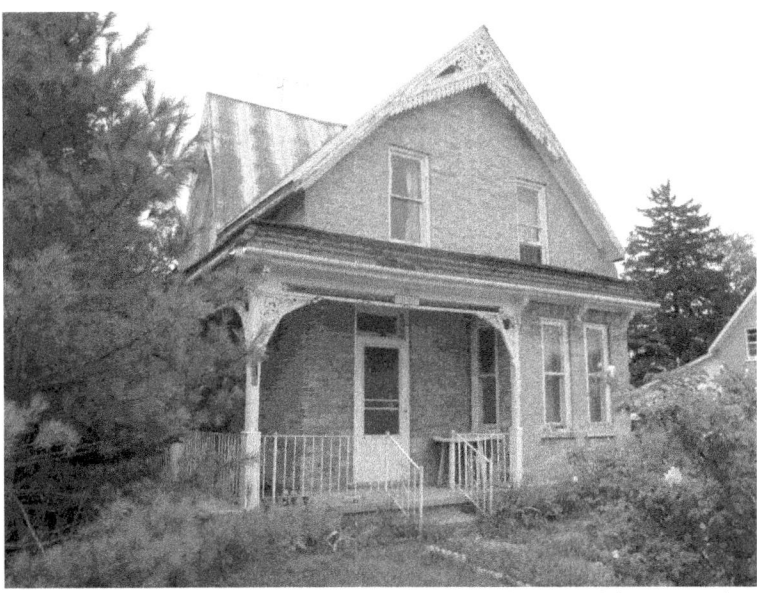

Gothic Revival – decorative Vergeboard on gable, metal roof, yellow brick, decorative brackets on verandah cornice

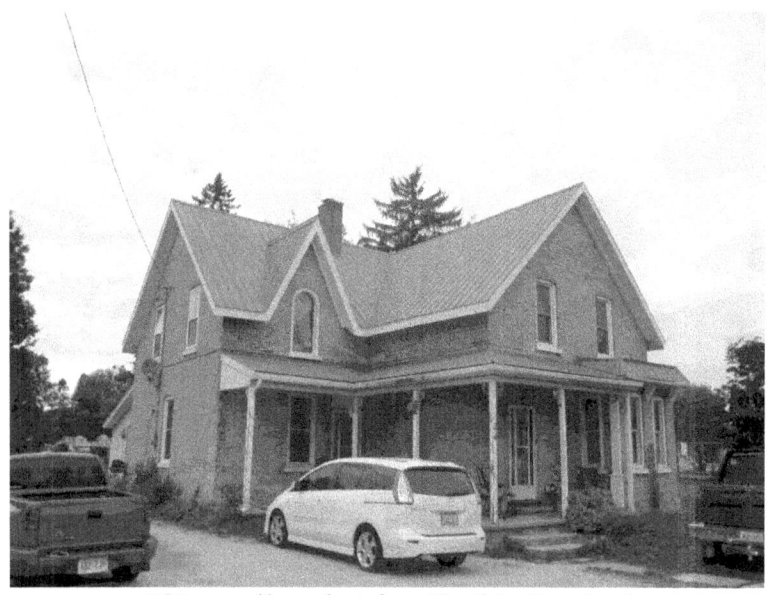

#24 – yellow brick – Gothic Revival

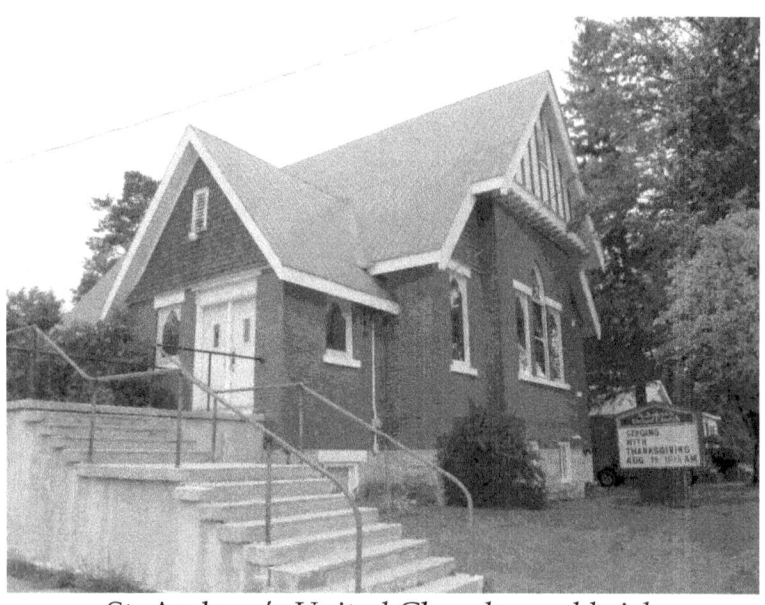

St. Andrew's United Church – red brick

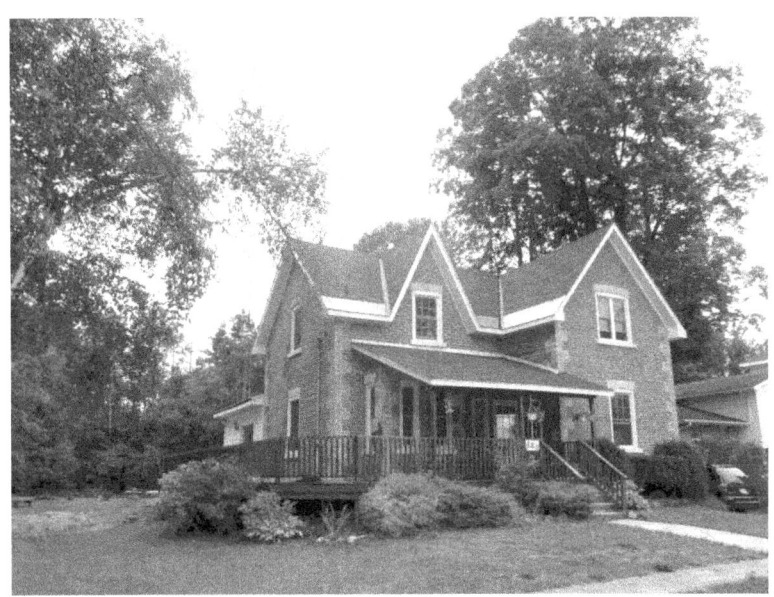

#480 – Gothic Revival – dichromatic brickwork, buff-coloured window hoods

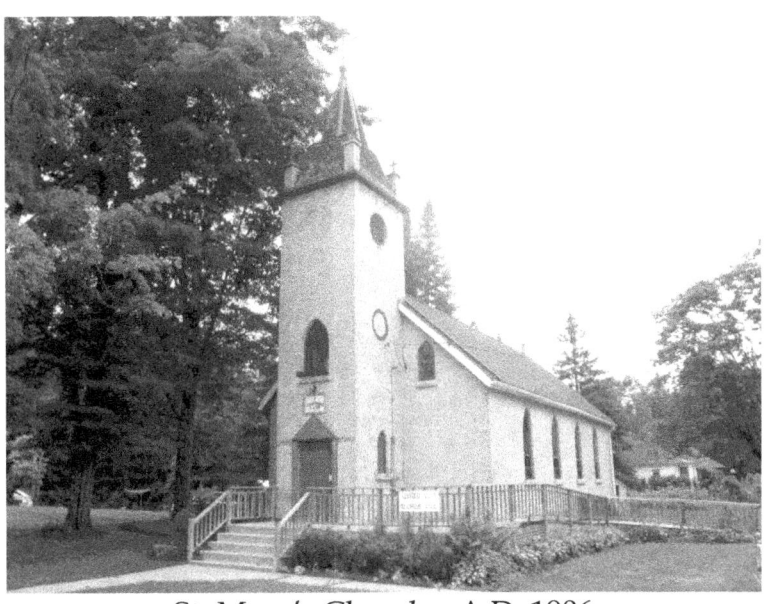

St. Mary's Church – A.D. 1906

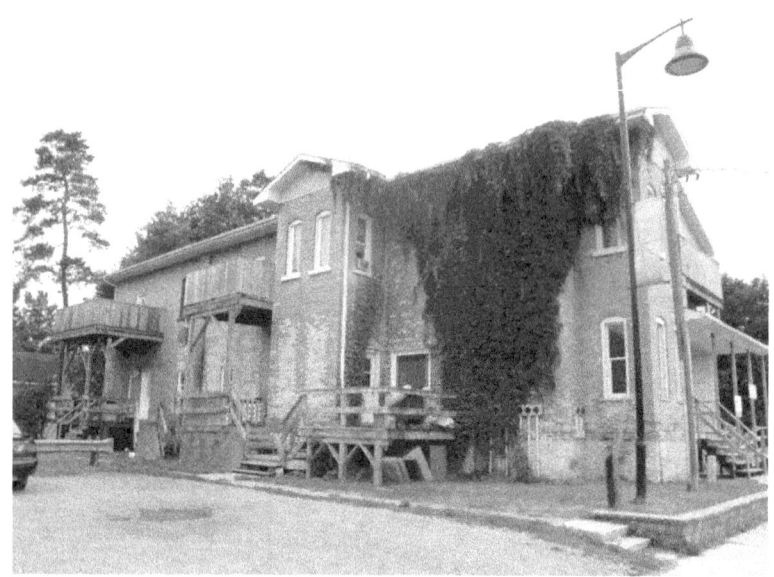

Yellow brick, partially vine covered – Italianate style

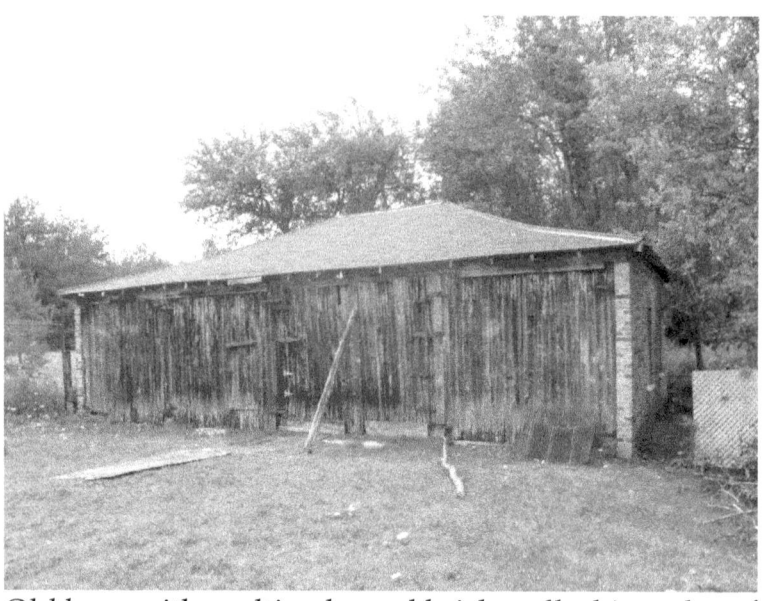

Old barn with multi-coloured brick walls, hipped roof

Sauble Beach

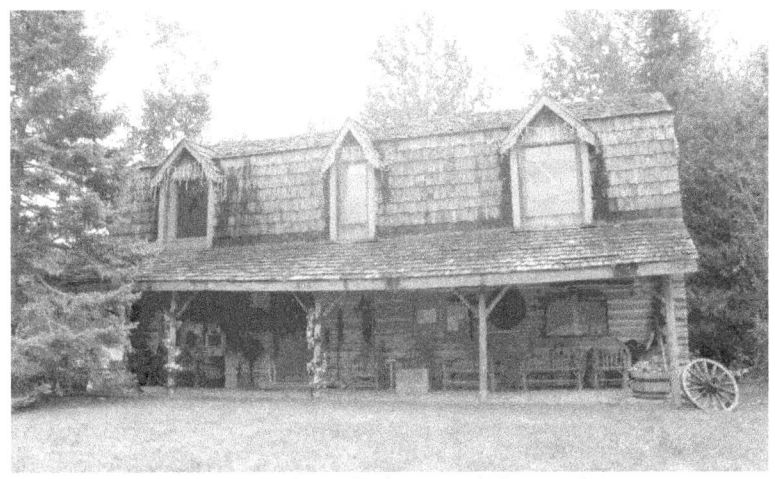

#808 – cedar shake roof, log cabin

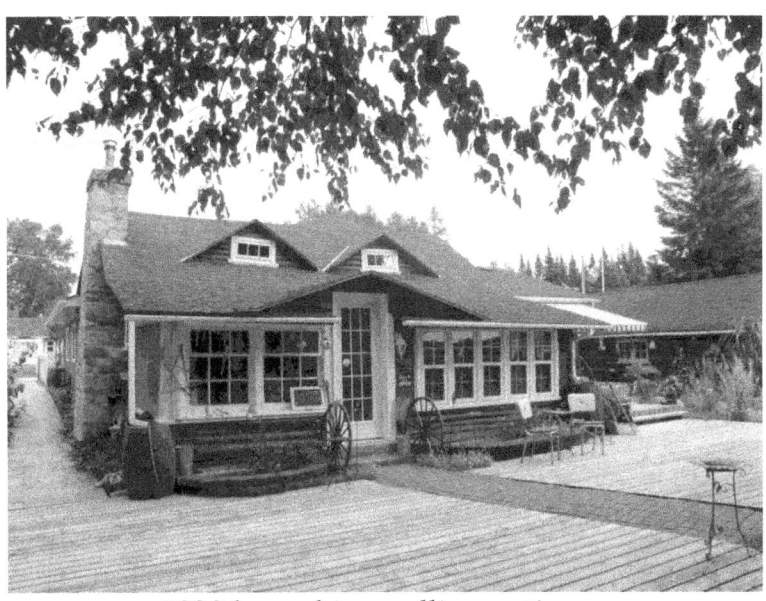

1930 log cabin – selling antiques

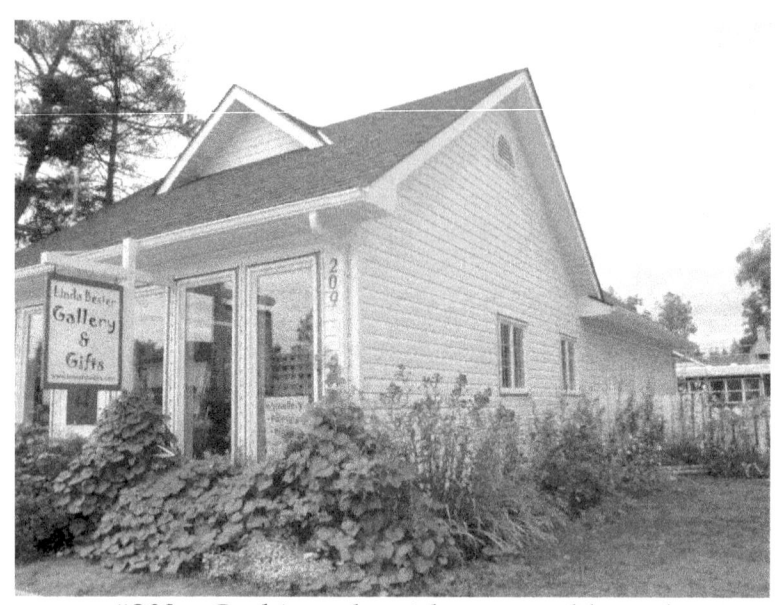

#209 – Gothic style with steep gable end

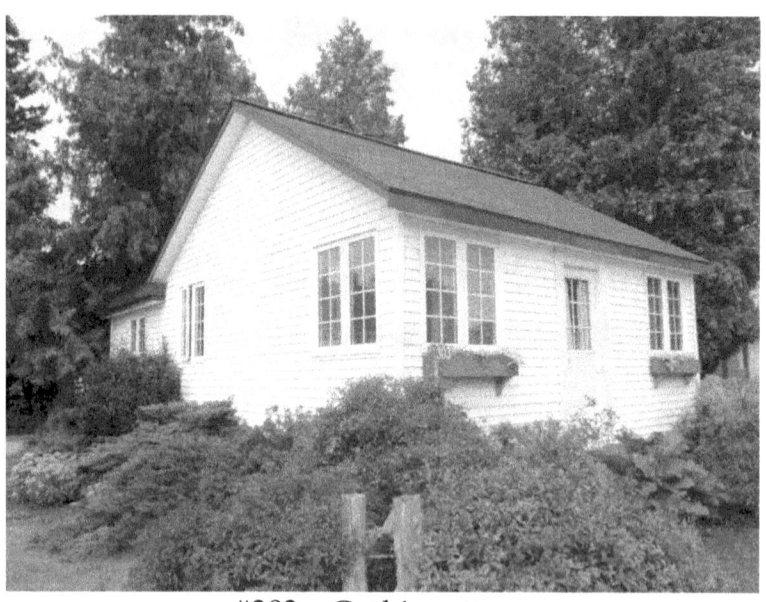

#303 – Gothic cottage

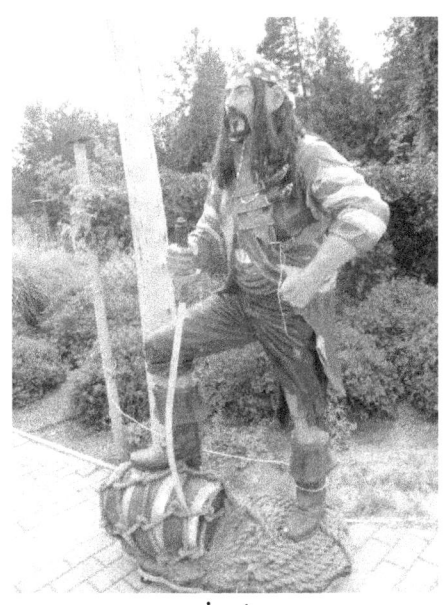

pirate

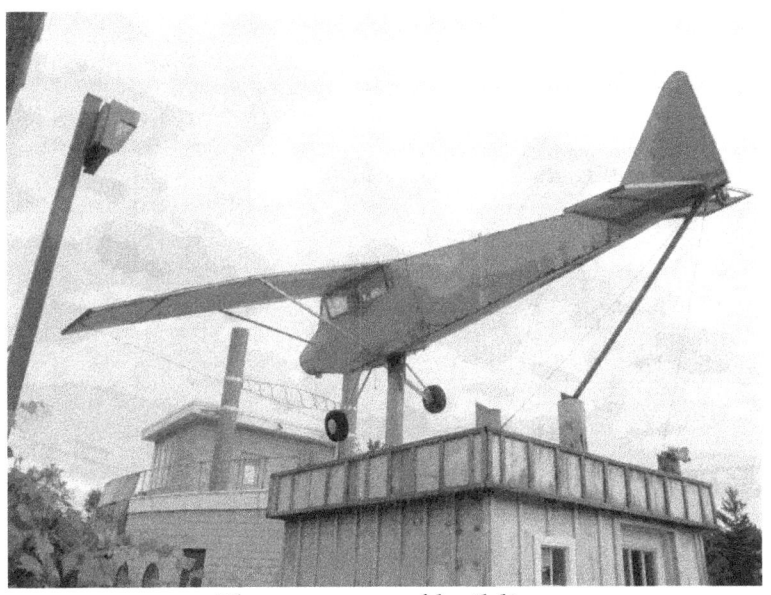

Plane on top of building

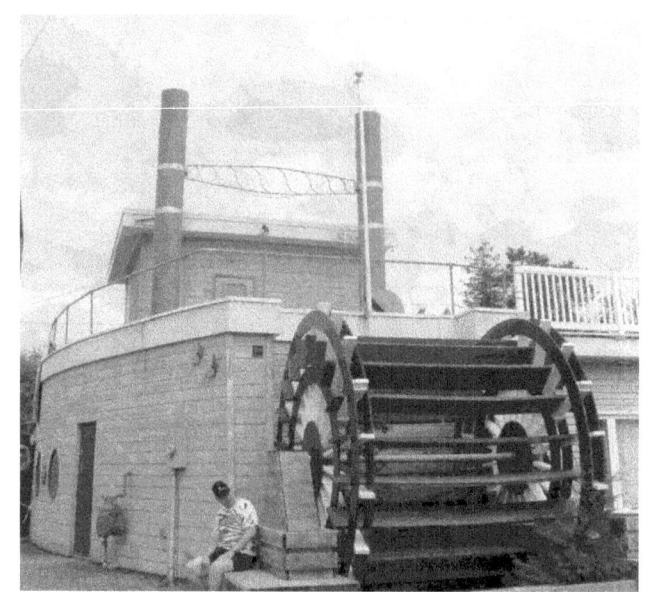

Paddle wheeler

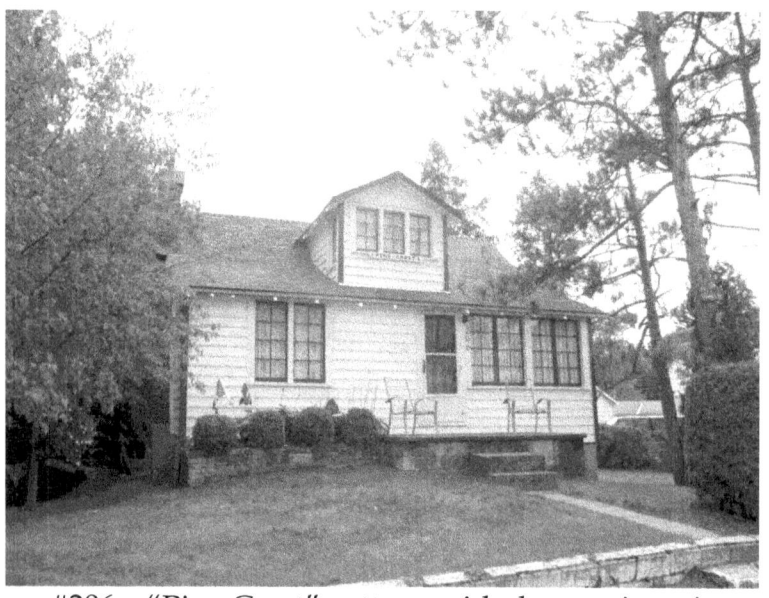

#206 – "Pine Crest" cottage with dormer in attic

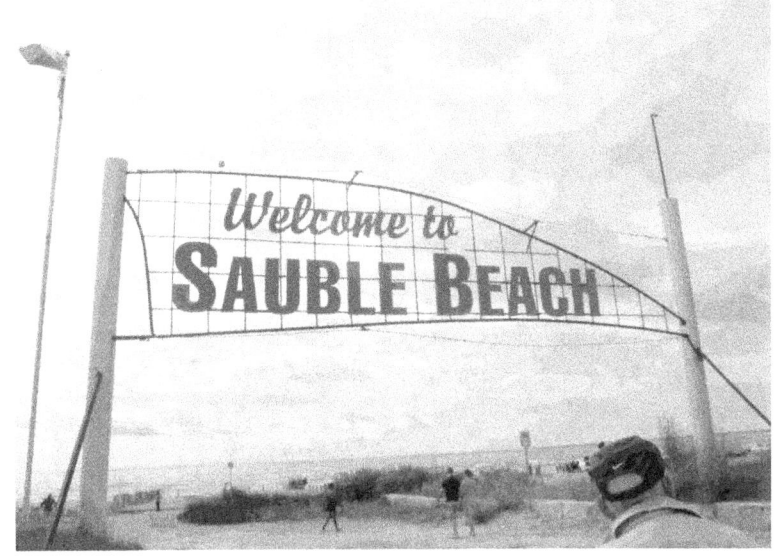

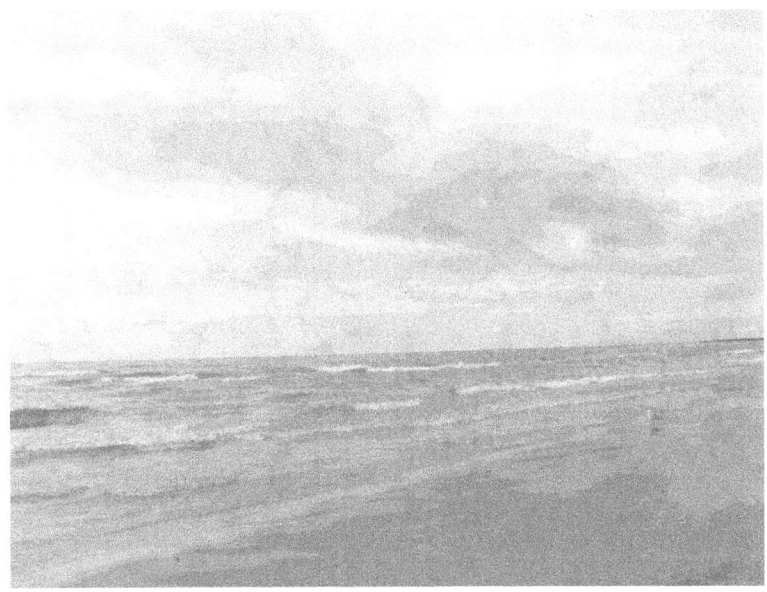

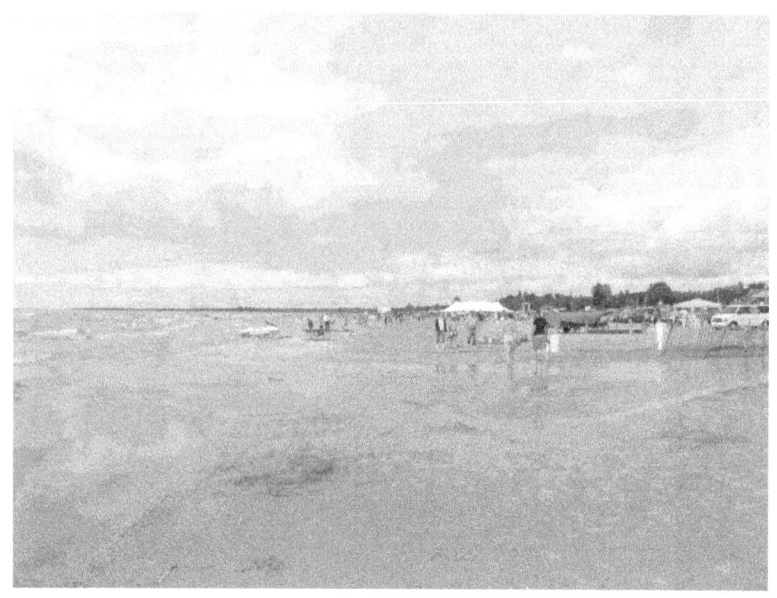

Shallow Lake

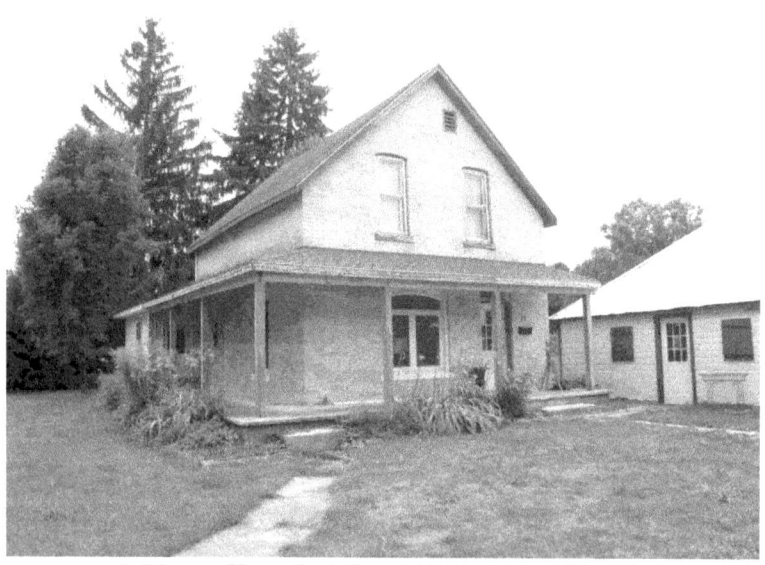

#47 – yellow brick – 1½ storey - Gothic

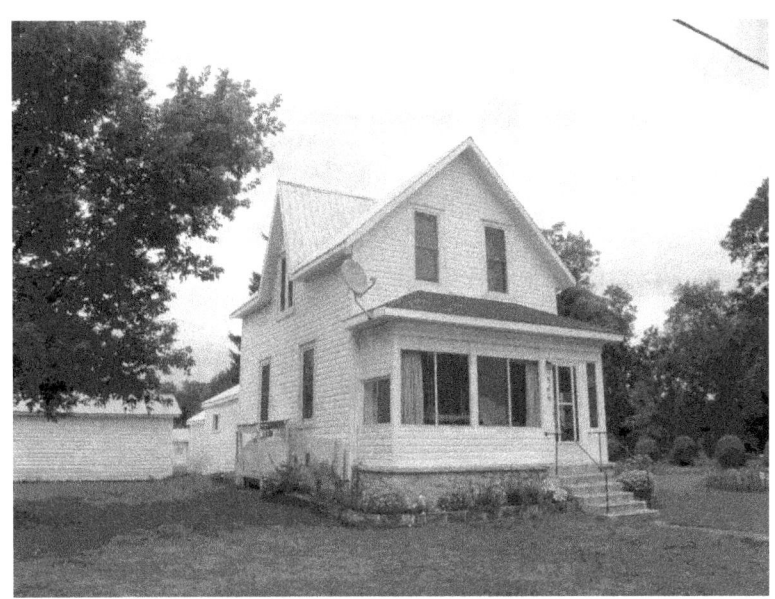

#346 – Gothic Revival

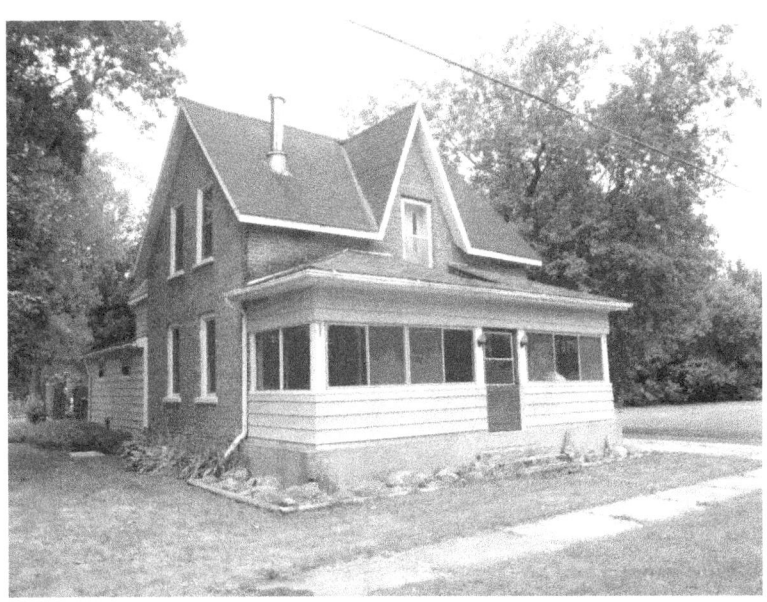

Gothic Revival – red brick – 1½ storey

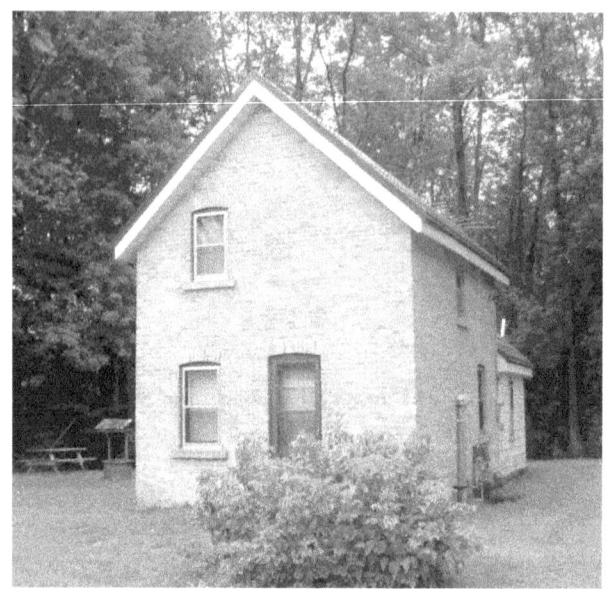
Gothic – yellow brick

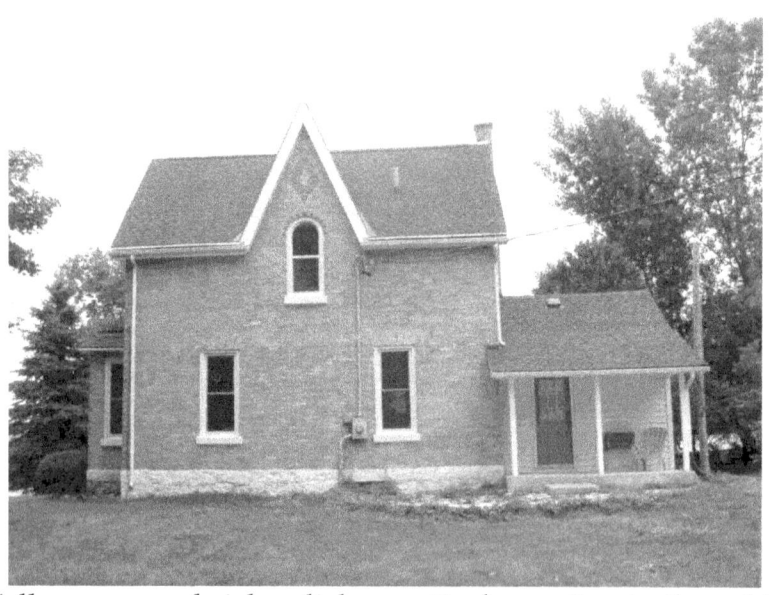
Yellow-orange brick – dichromatic decoration in the gable

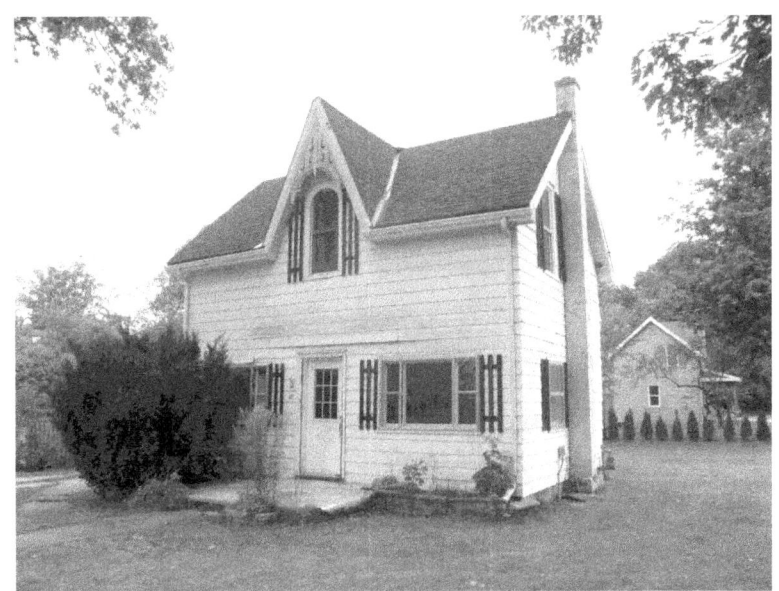

#35 – Gothic Revival – 1½ storey – Vergeboard trim on gable

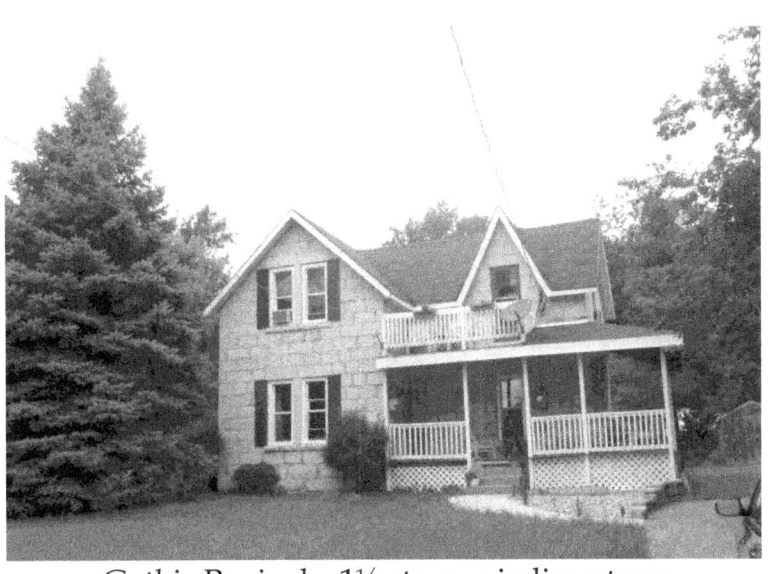

Gothic Revival – 1½ storeys in limestone

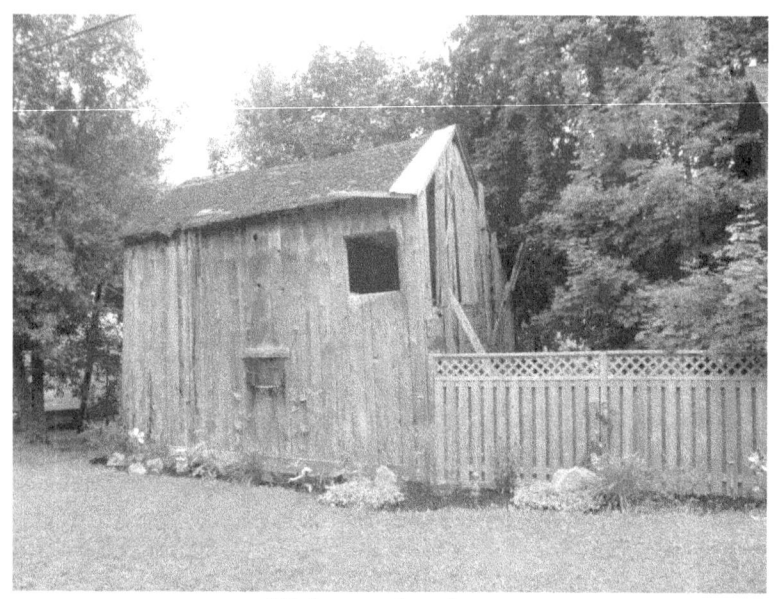
Old wooden barn

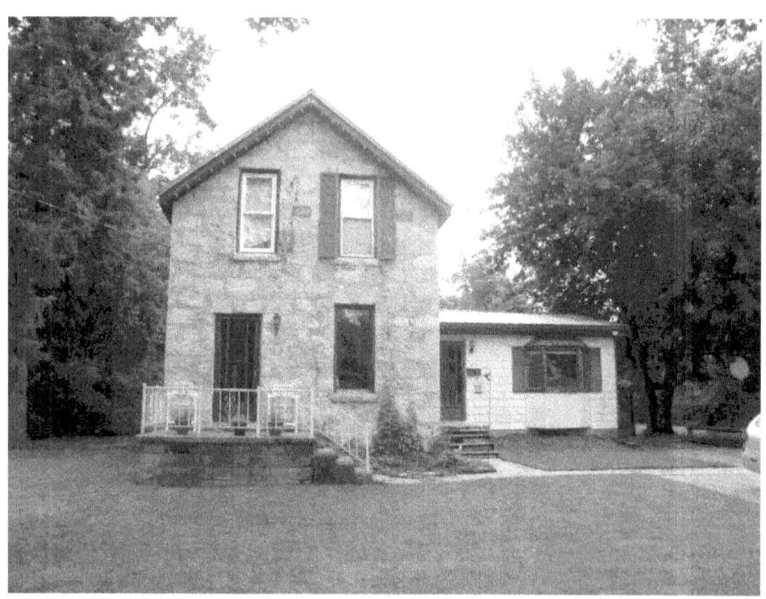
1½ storey limestone – Gothic style

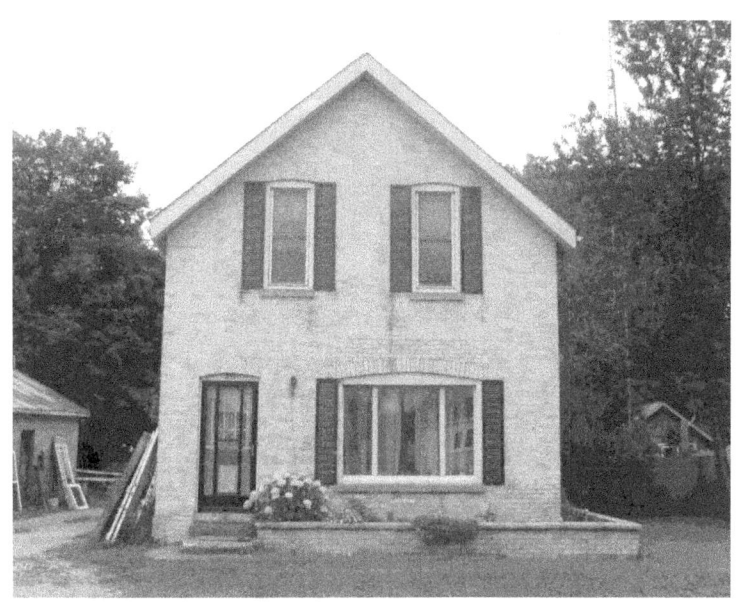

#233 - Yellow brick

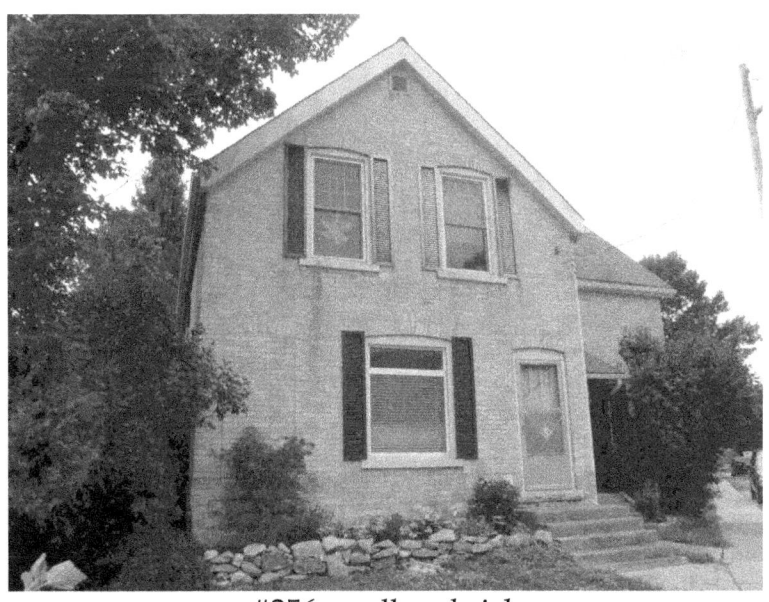

#256 – yellow brick

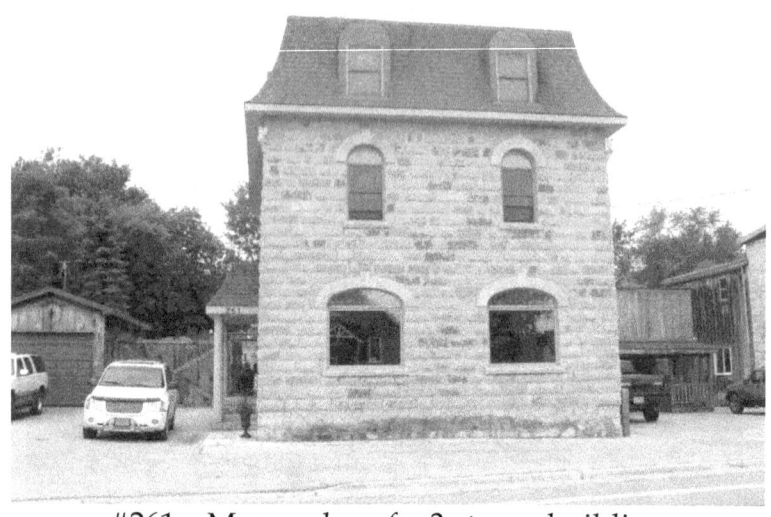

#261 – Mansard roof – 3 storey building

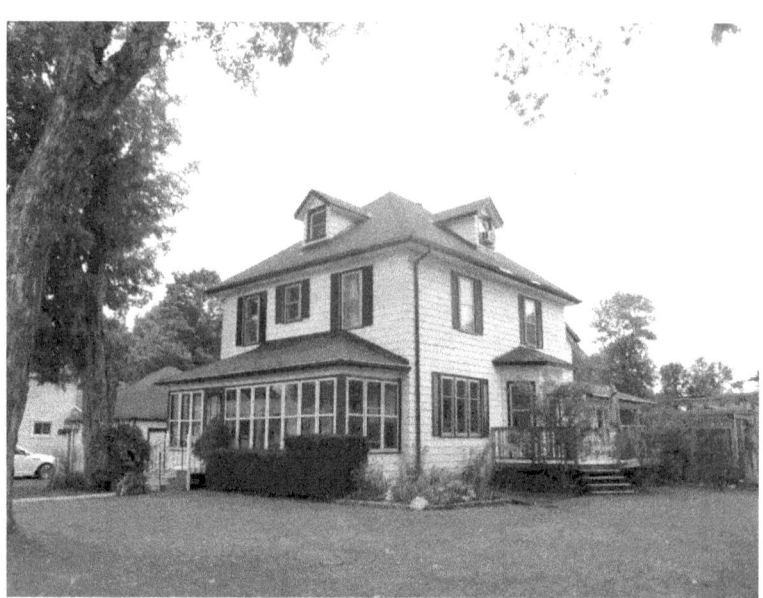

Italianate style with hipped roof, dormers in attic, bay window on side of house

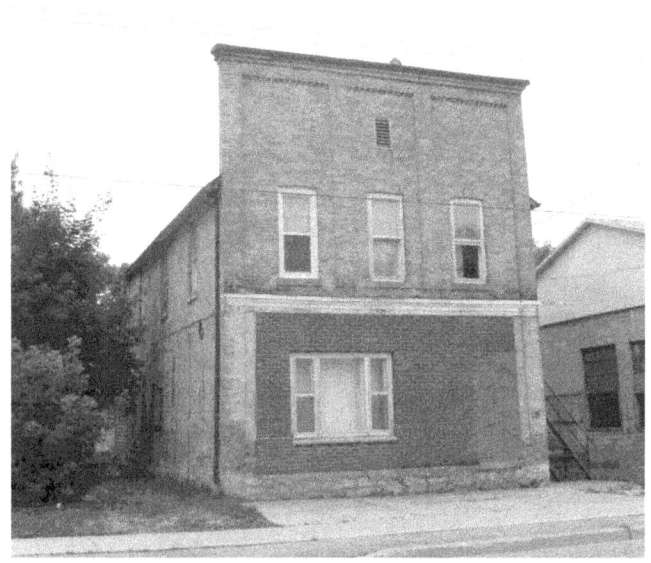

Yellow brick storefront

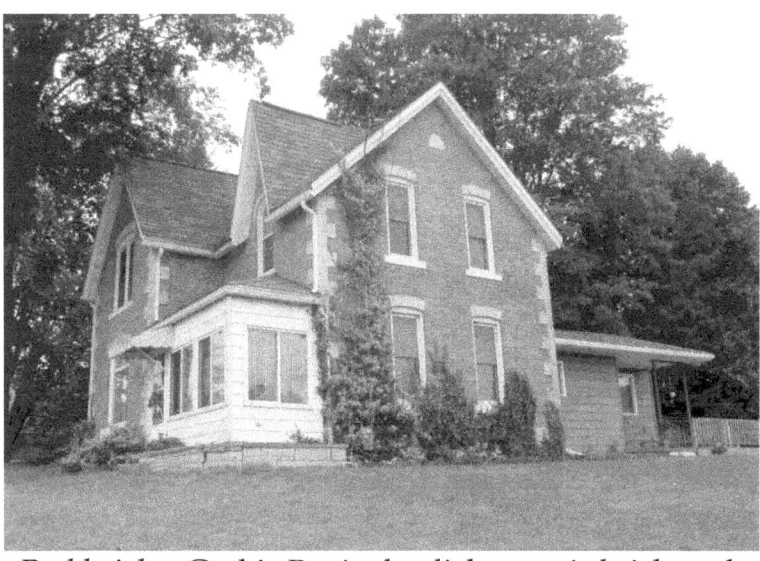

Red brick – Gothic Revival – dichromatic brickwork

Architectural Terms

Belvedere: (from the Italian "beautiful view") an architectural feature on a roof, in a garden or on a terrace that gives a beautiful view. Example: 559 Mill Street, Port Elgin	
Brackets: a decorative or weight-bearing structural element which forms a right angle with one side against a wall and the other under a projecting surface such as an eave or roof. Example: 559 Mill Street, Port Elgin	
Cobblestone architecture: Refers to the use of cobblestones embedded in mortar as a method for erecting walls on houses and commercial buildings. Example: 742 Mill Street, Port Elgin	
Cornice: originally the wooden overhang of the roof. With the use of stone, brick, iron and steel, the cornice is any projecting shelf at the top of a ceiling or roof. They can be very decorative. Example: 559 Mill Street, Port Elgin	
Cornice Return: decorative element on the end of a gable.	

Dentil Moulding: an even series of rectangles used as ornamental decoration in cornices. Example:	
Dichromatic brickwork: the use of two colours of brick, tile or slate to decorate a façade. Example: Shallow Lake	
Dormer: (French for "sleep") a gable end window that pierces through the plane of a sloping roof surface to create usable space in the top floor or attic of a building by adding headroom. Example: Green Street, Port Elgin	
Finial: ornament added to the top of a gable, pinnacle, canopy or spire – a Gothic element. Example: 464 Mill Street, Port Elgin	
Fretwork: interlaced decorative design resembling a bracket	
Frontispiece: a portion of the façade of a building, usually a centred doorway, that is slightly raised from the rest of the building, usually has extensive ornamentation. Frontispieces are usually Classical in design with white columned porches. Example:	

Gable: the triangular portion of a wall between the edges of a sloping roof. Example: Shallow Lake	
Hipped Roof: a roof where all sides slope downwards to the walls with no gables. Example: 503 Elgin Street, Port Elgin	
Keystones and Voussoirs: a voussoir is a wedge-shaped element used in building an arch. A keystone is the central stone that locks all the stones into position, allowing the arch to bear weight. A keystone is often enlarged and embellished. Example: downtown Port Elgin	
Lancet Window: a tall, narrow window with a pointed arch at its top. Example: Hepworth Hall	
Mansard Roof: This style was popularized by Francois Mansart (1598-1666), an accomplished architect of the French Baroque period and especially fashionable during the Second French Empire (1852-1870). This roof is almost flat on the top section, with two slopes on each of its sides with the lower slope at a steeper angle than the upper and having dormer windows. Example: Shallow Lake	

Pediment: a triangular section above the horizontal structure (entablature), typically supported by columns. The inside of the triangle is called the tympanum. Example: Port Elgin Public Library	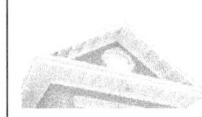
Quoin: masonry blocks at the corner of a wall, often a decorative feature, usually larger or of a different colour than the rest of the wall. Example: 535 Elgin Street, Port Elgin	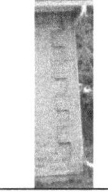
Vergeboards: also called bargeboards – hang from the projecting end of a roof and are often elaborately carved and ornamented. Example: 704 Gustavus Street, Port Elgin	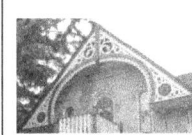
Window Hood: A **hood** is the piece found above window openings, usually of an ornate design, and covers the top third of the opening. Hoods are commonly placed above arched or curved openings on both windows and doors. Example: 481 Elgin Street, Port Elgin	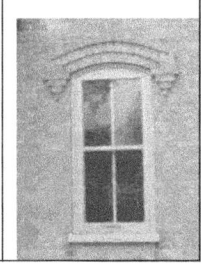

Port Elgin's Building Styles

Georgian, before 1860 – This style began with the British King Georges in the 18th century. These buildings have balanced facades around a central door, medium-pitched gable roofs, and small paned windows. Example:	
Regency Cottage, 1830-1860 – This style originated in England in 1815 and spread to Ontario later in the 19th century as British officers retired to Canada. It is a modest one-storey house with a low-pitched hip roof and has a symmetrical front façade. Example:	
Gothic Revival, 1830-1890 – These decorative buildings have sharply-pitched gables with highly detailed vergeboards, pointed-arch window openings, and dichromatic brickwork. It is a common style in Ontario. Example:	
Italianate, 1850-1900 – It has wide-bracketed eaves, belvederes, wrap-around verandahs. Example: 30 West Street	

Queen Anne, 1885-1900 – This style is distinguished by an irregular outline featuring a combination of an offset tower, broad gables, projecting two-storey bays, verandahs, multi-sloped roofs, and tall, decorative chimneys. A mixture of brick and wood is common. Windows often have one large single-paned bottom sash and small panes in the upper sash. Example: 184 Grand River Street North	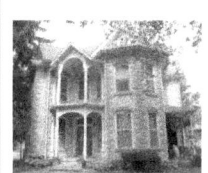
Edwardian, 1900-1930 – This style bridges the ornate and elaborate styles of the Victorian era and the simplified styles of the 20th century. Balanced facades, simple roof lines, dormer windows, large front porches, and smooth brick surfaces are its characteristics. Example: Willow Street	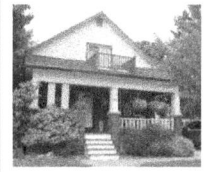

www.ingramcontent.com/pod-product-compliance
Lightning Source LLC
Chambersburg PA
CBHW071801200526
45167CB00017B/917